Combating Piracy in the Indian Ocean

Combating Piracy in the Indian Ocean

Cdr Shishir Upadhyaya (IN)

NATIONAL MARITIME FOUNDATION

Manas Publications
(We Convert Fighters into Writers)
New Delhi-110002 (INDIA)

MANAS PUBLICATIONS

(Publishers, Library Suppliers, Importers & Exporters)
4402/5-A, Ansari Road (Opp. HDFC Bank)
Darya Ganj, New Delhi-110 002 (INDIA)
Off. © 23260783, 23265523, Res. © 23842660
Fax: 011-23272766
E-mail: manaspublications@vsnl.com
manaspublications@yahoo.com

ISBN 978-81-7049-409-6
₹ 395/-

Designed at
Manas Publications

Printed in India at
IYN Graphics, Delhi
and published by Mrs Suman Lata for
Manas Publications, 4402/5-A, Ansari Road
(Opp. HDFC Bank),
Darya Ganj, New Delhi-110 002 (INDIA)

Contents

I dedicate this book lovingly, in the memory of my father,

Late Shri Hem Govind Upadhyaya

FOREWORD

The National Maritime Foundation is pleased to publish this monograph titled, 'Combating Piracy in the Indian Ocean,' by one of its Research Fellows; Commander Shishir Upadhyaya (IN). This wide-ranging study traces the history of piracy in the Indian Ocean, and the impact of its recrudescence in the 21st century, to pinpoint threats that confront India's maritime trade and security interests.

Cdr. Upadhyaya is a serving officer of the Indian Navy's Executive Branch. As a seaman and a specialist in Communications and Electronic Warfare, he has, over the years, gathered considerable experience of maritime security operations at sea. His narrative and analysis, thus, have an empirical basis and provide authentic insights into the practical difficulties and challenges faced by navies in combating piracy at sea, as well as in exercising naval surveillance over the vast Indian Ocean. He pertinently highlights the inadequacy of extant international laws as they apply to piracy, and the constraints inherent in the multi-national fabric of the global shipping industry in this context. These are some of the factors that, sadly, impinge on the unsatisfactory state of affairs which has led to a sense of grave insecurity amongst merchant mariners (and now even yachtsmen) plying the waters of the Indian Ocean.

Given the growing brazenness and audacity of Somalian pirates; their recent forays as far west as India's Lakshadweep Islands; and the obvious inadequacy of the endeavour by international navies, this monograph should come as a timely wake-up call to maritime stake-holders. After tracing the recent resurgence of piracy in our part of the world, the author examines the choices available to shipping companies and seafarers plying pirate-infested waters. He then surveys the ongoing naval initiatives, with special reference to the experience of the Indian Navy and Coast Guard in combating this menace. The author has clearly identified the impact of piracy on the Indian shipping industry and concludes his study with certain policy options for the Government of India.

This monograph will serve as an informative and easy to read 'primer' for policy makers and practitioners of maritime security, as well as those who have an interest in the ongoing fight against the disturbing phenomenon of piracy in the Indian Ocean.

Admiral Arun Prakash (Retd)
Chairman
National Maritime Foundation

PREFACE

Long considered outdated, piracy has returned in the 21st century to haunt the Indian Ocean. In many ways, little has changed since the times of the dreaded pirates, Henry Every and William Kidd who roamed the Indian Ocean in the 17th century. Even today, pirates continue to operate with impunity in gangs, attacking seafarers and capturing ships in the high seas. Significant developments of the 21st century such as globalisation, which has led to an increase in global seaborne trade and the increased automation onboard ships which has resulted in lesser manning of ships, have actually worsened the situation.

This monograph presents an overview of the various naval security initiatives in combating piracy (including salient operations of the Indian Navy) and the challenges being faced by them, with a view to understand the possible options before India.

I am grateful to all those who helped me in this project. I want to acknowledge Capt (Retd). JS Gill, Former DG Shipping India and Dr Sunil Kumar Aggarwal, Research Fellow NMF who helped me in understanding the legal aspects of piracy. I would like to thank M/s Jane Chan, Research Fellow RSIS, Singapore for her inputs in the naval initiatives in the Strait of Malacca. I also wish to thank the various representatives from the UK Maritime Trade Office (UKMTO), the Maritime Liaison Office (MARLO), NATO Shipping Centre (NSC) and the International Maritime Bureau (IMB) who I met during the Middle East Maritime Summit at Abu Dhabi in December 2010 and who provided me valuable insights into piracy in the Gulf of Aden. Last but not the least I thank my wife who motivated me to write this book.

As always, any omissions or errors in judgment in this work should be attributed to me alone. The views expressed in this book are mine and in no way do they reflect the official position of the Indian Navy or the Foundation.

I dedicate this book lovingly, in memory of my father who passed away in September 2010.

Commander Shishir Upadhyaya

Research Fellow

National Maritime Foundation

CHAPTER – I

INTRODUCTION

"The oceans are a domain increasingly beyond governmental control; they are vast and wild, where laws of nations mean little and where resilient pathogens of piracy and terrorism flourish"

—William Langewiesche[1]

***

Maritime piracy dates back as far as when ships first sailed into the high seas. The earliest Sumerian, Babylonian, Cretan and Egyptian records mention piracy. According to Sumerian records, Sumer was attacked by pirates from the Persian Gulf more than 4000 years ago. The sixth Babylonian King Hammurabi (between 1948-1905 BC) included a law against piracy in his famous code; the first known written law against piracy[2]. As maritime trade expanded so did piracy. In the Indian Ocean, geography played a key role in the growth of piracy. Both Arab and Malay pirates benefited from the strategic locations of the chokepoints in the Strait of Hormuz and the Strait of Malacca, respectively. Political instability of the time also aided the pirates who found safe havens in various locations along the coast. These very factors have led to a resurgence of piracy in the Gulf of Aden in the 21st century.

The period that lasted through the early 16th century and late 17th century is known as the Golden Age of Piracy. This was a period when loot and plunder of ships at sea was widespread, lucrative and threatening[3]. The Barbary Corsairs of the North Africa gained infamy as the worst pirates threatening Western shipping in the Mediterranean with savage violence. During this era, the Indian Ocean emerged as a notorious pirate's haunt in the late 17th century, when pirates like Henry Every and William Kidd preyed on British and Indian shipping from the Red Sea down to the Mozambique Channel and on the sea lanes between India and the Cape of Good Hope[4].

Several Western scholars – most recently Robert Kaplan in his book 'Monsoon' - have cited the instances of piratical attacks faced by Marco Polo and Ibn Battuta off the West coast of India in the 13th and 14th centuries[5], as evidence of piracy originating from India. However, it is opined that these attacks were actually attempts by the local fishermen community to keep off the transgressions by foreign traders or adventurers and hence not typically piratical attacks.

West Asia

During the 16th and 17th centuries, Indian trade with West Asia was adversely affected as many Indian vessels carrying *Haj* pilgrims or engaged in spice trade with the Arabs (these vessels were owned by the Gujarati business community), were pirated in the Red Sea. The most notable of incidents in this period, was that of the looting of the Indian vessel *Ganj-i-Sawai* in 1696 by the notorious pirate Henry Every, during the reign of Mughal Emperor Aurangzeb. The *Ganj-i-Sawai* was the largest ship of the Port of Surat. It was fitted out with 80 large guns and 400 matchlocks and was deemed so strong that it disdained the help of a convoy[6]. As the story goes, the vessel embarked with *Haj* pilgrims including the grand daughter of Aurungzeb and a number of members of the royal family was transiting the Strait of Bab-el-Mandap enroute from Saudi Arabia to Surat. The vessel was attacked by the pirate Henry Every, onboard his ship *Fancy* and despite the large guns and many armed soldiers onboard, the *Ganj-i-Sawai* was taken over without resistance.

It is said that the vessel was rummaged for a whole week by the crew of the *Fancy* who indulged in a horrible orgy. Over 52 Lakh (52,00,000.00) Rupees in Gold and Silver was taken as booty before the *Ganj-i-Sawai* was left to find its way to Surat as it best could[7]. When the news reached Emperor Aurangzeb, frustrated at his inability to apprehend the pirates he ordered all the English people in Surat to be put in prison; where they remained for over 11 months. It is said that Every, glutted with the booty from the *Ganj-i-Sawai*, soon retired. The news of his great booty spread from port to port[8] and was followed by the arrival of other pirates in the region intent on seeking new fortunes.

Southeast Asia

In Southeast Asia, the Strait of Malacca's location on the main commercial shipping route between India and China and the presence of numerous islets and river outlets which provided excellent hiding places made the region prone to piracy[9]

(Even today the challenges of maintaining constant surveillance in around the 17,500 islands that make up modern Indonesia are formidable). Moreover, during the Golden Age of piracy from the early 16th century to late 17th century, the Southeast Asian region suffered from political instability. The Malay Kingdom had been destroyed by the Portuguese in the early 16th century and replaced by weaker and smaller Sultanates. Thus, this period was marked by the advent of the Malay pirates viz the Buginese pirates of South Sulawesi, the Orang Laut pirates of Riau Island and the Sea Dayak pirates operating from Borneo Island. These pirate groups sailed as far West as Singapore and as far North as the Philippines in search of opportune targets.

Piracy in the Southeast Asian region continued into the 19th century even after it had declined elsewhere in the West. In the early 19th century, when the Sultan of Johar ruled over the Riau Archipelago and the Sultan of Aceh ruled Northwestern Sumatra, piracy was rampant since both the rulers had little control over their subjects[10]. Moreover, with the arrival of the colonial powers viz Portuguese, Dutch and English; the volume of maritime trade – mainly in Opium and Spices - had increase manifold through the Strait of Malacca providing lucrative targets for the local pirates.

The most notorious Malay pirate was Raga who operated in the Makassar Strait for more than 17 years. In 1813, he captured three British ships and brutally killed their Masters with his bare hands. According to some accounts, by 1830 Raga had captured more than 40 European ships and executed their masters and crew[11]. The British forces made several unsuccessful attempts to curb the transgressions of Raga in the straits, however they were constrained by lack of adequate warships. Eventually, in 1830, the British and Dutch naval forces joined hands at combating pirates, dividing the straits along the Anglo-Dutch line (this line is currently the maritime border between Malaysia and Indonesia). By 1870 piracy in the Indian Ocean had greatly declined, aided to a great extent by the advent of steam propulsion which gave the merchantmen an advantage over the pirates of the day[12].

Emergence of Piracy in the 21st Century

Following a period of peaceful global maritime trade that lasted well over a century, piracy in the world, first re-emerged towards the end of the 20th century in the Strait of Malacca, a result of the financial crisis in the region. By 2004, the number of attacks on ships transiting the Strait of Malacca region had reached a record number of 157, almost half of the global total of 329! The Strait of Malacca was declared as the world's top piracy hotspot by the International Maritime Bureau (IMB) and placed in the war risk zone by Lloyd's War Committee, resulting in the levy of additional insurance surcharge for ships transiting the Straits. This prompted the Southeast Asian littoral states; Singapore, Indonesia, Thailand and Malaysia to launch the naval anti-piracy patrols codenamed Operation MALSINDO. Piracy has since declined in the Strait of Malacca, though it still requires the constant surveillance efforts of four navies.

Just when piracy started declining in the Strait of Malacca region, a new 'hotspot' emerged in the Gulf of Aden region. This was the manifestation of a greater problem in Somalia, which has not seen a central government since January 1991[13]. The scale and range of attacks by the Somali pirates has never been witnessed since the times of the Barbary corsairs between the 16th and the 18th century. Equally unprecedented has been the response of the global community and currently a majority of the G20 navies are deployed in the Gulf of Aden on anti-piracy patrols.

Piracy continues to challenge navies and the shipping industry in the 21st century as it did in the past between the 16th and 18th century. The Indian Ocean region has emerged as the global 'Centre of Gravity' of piracy accounting for a vast majority of the piracy incidents worldwide. This poses a huge challenge for India, the only significant resident maritime power in the Indian Ocean. This monograph discusses the resurgence of piracy in the 21st century in the Strait of Malacca and the Gulf of Aden regions of the Indian Ocean and brings out specific policy options for India. The monograph is divided into seven chapters. Chapter Two examines the various strategic imperatives of the IOR, the prevalent maritime security scenario and the nature of the evolving shipping industry. Chapter Three of the monograph provides an overview of the various international laws on piracy as also the extant India laws on the subject. Chapter Four discusses the challenges of piracy in the Gulf of Aden, including the various security initiatives in the region and the emerging trends.

The Fifth chapter deals with piracy in the Strait of Malacca and the scope for participation by the Indian navy in the ongoing security initiatives by the Southeast Asian littoral states. Chapter Six provides an account of the role played by India in combating piracy in the IOR and highlights the experiences of the Indian navy and Indian coast guard in combating piracy in the IOR. Finally, in Chapter Seven the key findings of the monograph are discussed in the form of various policy options for India. Throughout, the monograph seeks to put into context the role of the Indian Navy and other stakeholders viz the shipping industry and the international maritime organisations in combating piracy.

Article 101 of the 1982 United Nations Convention on the Law of the Sea (UNCLOS) defines piracy as follows:-

- Any illegal acts of violence or detention, or any act of depredation, committed for private ends by the crew or the passengers of a private ship or a private aircraft, and directed:
  - o on the high seas, against another ship or aircraft, or against persons or property on board such ship or aircraft;
  - o against a ship, aircraft, persons or property in a place outside the jurisdiction of any State;
- Any act of voluntary participation in the operation of a ship or of an aircraft with knowledge of facts making it a pirate ship or aircraft;
- Any act inciting or of intentionally facilitating an act described in sub-paragraph (a) or (b).

The International Maritime Organization (IMO) reports piracy based on the above definition. However, the International Maritime Bureau (IMB) defines piracy as the act of boarding any vessel with an intent to commit theft or any other crime and with an intent or capacity to use force in furtherance of that act.

In this monograph, the IMB definition which is wider in scope than the IMO definition has been used.

Endnotes

1. *William Langewiesche.* Anarchy at Sea. www.wesjones.com. Accessed on May 24, 2010.

2. James Wombwell. 'The Long War Against Piracy; Historical Trends. 'Occasional paper 32. Combat Studies Institute Press US Army Combined Arms Centre Fort Leavenworth, Kansas.

3. Virginia Lunford. 'What Makes Piracy Work,' USN Institute, Proceedings. December 2008.

4. Angus Konstam. 'Scourge of the Seas; Buccaneers, Pirates and Privateers.' p 107. Osprey Publishing Ltd, UK, 2000.

5. Robert Kaplan. 'Monsoon - The Indian Ocean and the Future of American Power.' P 298. Random House, New York,2010.

6. Col John Biddulph. 'The Pirates of Malabar.'p 26. Lancer International. ISBN 81-7062-171-2.

7. Ibid. p 27.

8. Ibid. p 32.

9. http://en.wikipedia.org/wiki/Piracy_in_the_Strait_of_Malacca (accessed on July 15, 2009).

10. Note ii ibid. p 98.

11. Ibid. p 99.

12. Note v, ibid, p 300.

13. Peter Lehr. 'The Threat of Piracy and Maritime Terrorism to International Shipping: Developing Effective Measures of Mitigation.' TRANSEC Conference, Mumbai. September 2009.

CHAPTER – II

THE INDIAN OCEAN REGION: STRATEGIC IMPERATIVES

"The Asian energy SLOCs originating in the Persian Gulf take the oil and gas laden ships, through the Iran dominated Strait of Hormuz, around strife-torn Sri Lanka through the Malacca Straits or Indonesia's archipelagic sea lanes into the disputed waters of the South China Sea. During this passage, they run the gauntlet of piracy, maritime terrorism and inter-state conflict. In ensuring their safety lies a significant convergence of interests and scope for cooperation between Asia's energy consumers."

—Admiral (Retired) Arun Prakash[1]

***

The Indian Ocean Region (IOR) is commonly described as stretching from East Africa to Tasmania and from Asia to Antarctica. Nearly 100,000 ships transit the Indian Ocean each year along the 'Equatorial Pendulum' or the main shipping route carrying one third of the world's bulk cargo, half of the containers and two-thirds of the oil. The geographical position of the Indian Ocean and its strategic waterways provide the shortest and most economical lines of communication linking it to the Atlantic and the Pacific Ocean. The Indian Ocean has nine important choke points namely; Suez Canal, Strait of Hormuz, Strait of *Bab-el-Mandap*, Strait of Malacca, Lombok Strait, Sunda Strait, Six Degree Channel, Nine Degree Channel and the route via Cape of Good Hope to the Mozambique Channel. These choke points, as brought out earlier make the India Ocean vulnerable to piracy and armed attacks on ships and therefore it is imperative that the choke points are free from trouble at all time.

The political map of the Indian Ocean comprises 56 littoral and hinterland states. 36 states have access to the Indian Ocean. The IOR houses one third of the world's population whereas it has only a quarter of the world's landmass. Some other salient aspects of the IOR are as follows:-

- The IOR holds 65% of the known reserves of strategic raw materials, including one third of natural gas and more than half of the world's oil reserves. Australia, which is washed by the Indian Ocean to its West, holds about 40% of the world's known Uranium reserves.
- About 95% of the world's cyber-space traffic is carried in the undersea cables that span the Indian Ocean seabed.
- The world's fastest growing economies such as India and Vietnam and the richest countries such as Australia co-exist with some of the poorest countries of the world such as Somalia and Afghanistan.
- The IOR is the *de facto* home of global terrorism with the world's leading terrorist groups present and active in the many regional states and states such as Pakistan covertly aiding and abetting subversive elements.

- The IOR is also the centre of gravity of piracy and many trans-national crimes, with the majority of the pirate attacks occurring in its sea lanes.
- The IOR is the locus of 70% of the world's natural disasters. Majority of these having occurred in Southeast Asia.

Overview of the Maritime Security Scenario in the IOR

In recent decades the exploitation of the seas and oceans globally, has reached unprecedented levels, driven by the rapidly rising demand for natural resources on land[2]. States and corporations are turning more than ever to the sea for transportation, energy, water, food, minerals, waste disposal, etc. The impact of these pressures more than anywhere can be witnessed in the IOR, which has the highest density of population (with over a third of the world's population living on one-fourth the land mass). Adding to the increasing pressure on the sea is the spill over of trans-national criminal activities including terrorist activities, which now face increasing prosecution on land.

Another important factor affecting the security of ships at sea is the dramatic increase in shipping traffic. Seaborne trade has doubled every decade since 1945 and shipbuilding tonnage has doubled since 1990[3]. Over 90 % of global trade is seaborne; supported by a massive infrastructure of almost 93,000 ships with 1.25 million seamen bound for three thousand different ports[4].

Maritime Terrorism: Currently, a wide spectrum of threats are predominantly present in the IOR ranging from poaching activities and armed robberies/ attacks on ships at the lower end of the spectrum to large-scale maritime terrorist attacks at the other end. Majority of the global hotspots for piracy are located in the IOR. The world's leading terrorist groups such as the *Al Qaeda, Lashkar-e-Tayyiba (LeT)* and the *Jemmah Islamiyah* (JI) are known to be operating in IOR. All these groups are known to have maritime experts in their cadres and have demonstrated their capability to carry out maritime attacks in the past. The *Al Qaeda* was responsible for the attack on the French tanker Limburg and the USS Cole, both of which occurred in the Gulf of Aden in 2002. In 2004, the JI was involved in the bombing of the Philippine *Super Ferry 14,* considered to be the most destructive act of terrorism in maritime history and the fourth most serious terrorist attack since 9/11.[5] More recently, the LeT was responsible for the November 26, 2008 attack in Mumbai. Needless to say, the maritime security scenario in IOR is tense and there is a clear threat of the terrorist groups linking up with pirates. Even though much evidence is currently not available in this regard, the threat has been accentuated by the increasing pressure on terror outfits on land due to the global war on terror unleashed by the USA post 9/11.

Piracy: In the IOR piracy has emerged in the 21st century in two regions; the Gulf of Aden region off Somalia and the Strait of Malacca region. Both these hotspots flank the extremities of the 'Equatorial Pendulum' that cuts across the Indian Ocean and through which over 100,000 ships transit annually. Security at both points in the chain is paramount for smooth functioning of the global supply chain.

The attacks on ships can be categorised into minor and major attacks. Minor attacks include attacks on ships in ports or anchorages leading to thefts of ship's gear, onboard fittings, crew belongings, etc. At the other end, major attacks include outright theft of ships, hijackings, stealing of cargo, kidnapping and other violent attacks on crew, etc. A graph depicting the IMB record of piracy incidents worldwide between 2000 and 2010 is shown below.

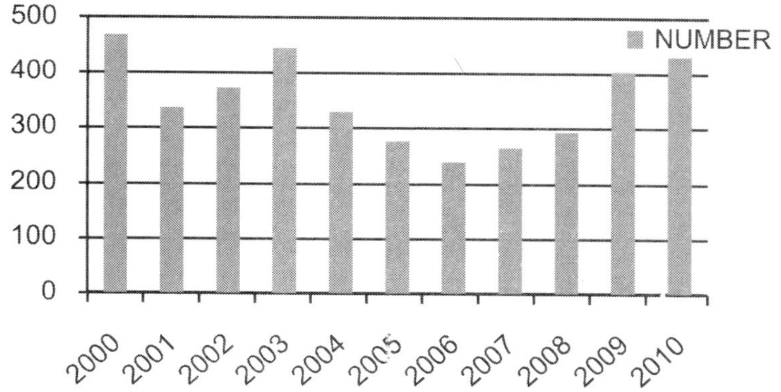

Source: *International Maritime Bureau*

Fig. 2.1 Record of Piracy Incidents Worldwide 2000 –2010

The majority of piracy incidents worldwide between 2000 to 2010 can be attributed to piracy in the IOR alone. The first part of the graph; for the period 2000 to 2006 is largely a result of piracy in the Strait of Malacca. However, these numbers began to decline post 2004 when Operation MALSINDO was launched by the Southeast littorals. The steep increase in piracy since 2006 is mainly due to the spurt in piracy attacks by Somali pirates in the Gulf of Aden region.

Drivers for Piracy

One of the key drivers for piracy has been the increase in seaborne trade as a result of globalisation in the recent decades. Other contributing factors are the rise of the open registers or Flag of Convenience (FOC) ships as the preferred choice for registration of ships, increased automation onboard ships which has resulted in lower manning requirements and the evolution of the shipping industry as a multinational enterprise. These aspects are discussed in the following paragraphs.

Open Registers or FOC Ships

The number of ships operating under open registers has been on the rise. In the 1950s, approximately 4% of the world's merchant fleet was registered under FOC. On July 01, 2009 the tonnage of FOC ships stood at 657.9 million dwt; representing a share of 55.1% of the world total (300 tons and above)[6]. The top ten countries offering open registers are Panama, Liberia, Marshall Islands, the Bahamas, Malta, Cyprus, Antigua and Barbuda, Bermuda, Saint Vincent and

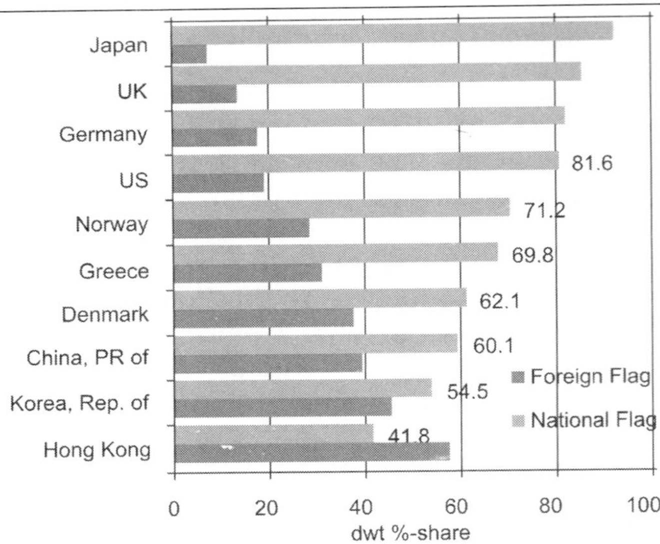

Source: *ISL Institute of Shipping Economics and Logistics*

Fig. 2.2 Share of Foreign and National Flag Shipping of Top Ten Countries.

Cayman Islands. Recently, land locked countries such as Bolivia and Mongolia have also entered the business of open registers. The top ten countries of the world in terms of shipping tonnage and their share of national and foreign tonnage is depicted in the adjoining graph. Except for Hong Kong all the counties have more than half of their shipping tonnage under foreign flags.

The motivation for choosing a foreign flag varies from country to country and vessel type; the primary reason being reduction in operating costs. Thus, ships under FOC are less likely to invest in onboard security measures. In accordance with Article 91 of the UNCLOS, 1982,

"Ships have the nationality of the state whose flag they are entitled to fly."

This implies that the flag state is responsible for the overall conduct of the vessel in an international environment[7]. However, a large majority of the FOC states lack the capability to ensure security of their ships and are accused of having low safety standards and a poor record of inspections[8]. This factor has a direct impact on the traditional task of navies; that of providing trade protection, since navies would have no legal right to convoy shipping owned by another state[9]. The net result of more than half of the world's ships being FOC ships is that the task of providing security to the entire global shipping industry has to be shouldered by the handful of navies currently deployed on anti piracy patrols. Needless to say, this is a formidable task.

Multinational Nature of the Shipping Industry

Global shipping can be divided into liner and tramp shipping. The former includes ships operating on fixed schedules and routes and are mostly owned by large multinational conglomerates. Tramp ships normally ply on various routes moving from Port to Port in search of cargo. In recent decades, driven by the need for economising on operating costs and optimising the capacity, shipping liners have resorted to horizontal integration of their assets, operations and markets. This has led to the formation of consortia and strategic or global alliances.

Consortia: Consortia are agreements between liner shipping companies, aimed primarily at operating joint services through technical, operational or commercial coordination such as joint use of vessels, marketing organisations, etc.

Strategic or Global Alliances: Strategic alliances emerged in 1990s with shipping lines looking to provide combined services on various routes. This was done to increase efficiency and to ensure better utilisation of vessels. These included joint vessel-route assignments, sailing schedules, optimising the type and size of vessels to be employed, etc; such that each participant's services were integrated into one operating system[10]. Two salient examples are, the Grand Alliance comprising of Hapag Lloyd, MISC, NYK, OOCL, P&O Nedlloyd and the New World Alliance of APL, Hyundai and MOL.

The future trend in shipping is towards mega consortiums of shipping lines that achieve huge economies of scale and synergy of efforts by merger of their operations. It is forecast that the shipping lines of the future could evolve into a few – perhaps one or two - large multiple member alliances operating the 'Equatorial Pendulum' which is the main global shipping route cutting across the Indian

Ocean from the West to the East. Eventually, it is envisaged that the liner shipping of the future will transform into worldwide 'maritime pipelines' no different from the roads and rails infrastructure on land. Such 'pipelines' would be operated by neutral non shipping bodies which may even be financial institutions[11] such as Banks.

Today's merchant ships are akin to floating multinational enterprises. For example, a ship owned by a German Business house could be registered in Panama, managed by a Greek company, insured by an American company, re-insured by a UK company, chartered to a Korean client for carrying Chinese cargo and manned by crew from India, Bangladesh and Philippines! Over 10 different countries involved in one ship! Thus, as the shipping industry evolves into fewer and larger cooperative multinational enterprises, the burden of security for shipping will have to be shared by various states participating in the multiple member alliances. Accordingly, naval security initiatives will have to evolve into cooperative security mechanisms to address the security concerns.

Conclusion

The IOR has emerged as the global hub for piracy, transnational crimes and maritime terrorism. The increased pressure on land based non state actors post 9/11 and the rapid increase in maritime activities - fuelled by the rising demand for natural resources on land - have resulted in a spill over of crimes from land to sea. Further, the increase in shipping traffic in recent decades, rise in number of FOC ships - without a genuine link to their flag state - and the evolving multinational nature of the shipping industry have led to a lack of propensity on part of the shipping industry to invest in security. This is marked by a tendency on part of the shipping industry to 'pass the buck.'

As a result of these factors there is increased pressure on the navies to provide security at sea. Further, due to the multinational nature of the shipping industry, there is also a need for navies to evolve cooperative security mechanisms. Perhaps, signs of this evolution can be seen in the Gulf of Aden where more than 20 warships from over 14 navies are currently operating on anti-piracy patrols.

Endnotes

1. Admiral (retd) Arun Prakash, Former Chief of the Indian Navy at the IISS-JIIA Conference 2-4 June 2008, Tokyo, Japan.
2. 'Martin N Murphy. Contemporary Piracy and Maritime Threats' Adelphi Paper 388, IISS. p 75.
3. Bruce A. Elleman, *et al.* Piracy and Maritime Crimes, Historical and Modern Case Studies, Chapter V. Naval War College Press, Newport, Rhode Island, USA.
4. Ibid.
5. Dr Peter Chalk, "Maritime Dimension of International Security", p. 49., RAND, USA.
6. Shipping Statistics and Market Review. Volume 53, NO 11/ 2009. ISL Institute of Shipping Economics and Logistics. www.isl.org. Accessed on July 24, 2010.
7. Manav Sehgal. ' Open Registers: A Necessity or Mere Convenience.' *Maritime Affairs*, A Journal of the National Maritime Foundation, Volume 6, Number 1, Summer 2010.
8. Ibid. Note vii.
9. GS Khurana, 'Maritime Security in the Indian

Ocean: Convergence Flus Cooperation Equals Resonance.' *Strategic Affairs*, Volume 28)3, July-September (2004).

10. Indian Maritime Landscape, Background Note, February 2008. KPMG and CII Study.

11. Containerisation, Multimodal transport and Business Economics by Dr KV Hariharan. Jul7 2007, Shroff Publishers, Mumbai.

CHAPTER – III

LEGAL ASPECTS OF MARITIME PIRACY

" Piracy suspects should be brought to justice, not simply let go or left to die."

—Ban Ki-moon[1]

***

Definition of Piracy

Even though piracy has been around for centuries, ironically, the world is yet to evolve comprehensive laws for prosecution of pirates. More than 2000 years ago, the famous Roman philosopher, statesman, lawyer, political theorist, and constitutionalist, Marcus Tullius Cicero defined piracy as *hostis humani generis,* meaning "enemies of the human race." Since then piracy has been internationally regarded as a universal crime or *sui generis*. However, today when prosecuting the pirates in court rooms - rather than hanging them from the yardarm - is the approach of 'civilised' societies, the international laws are found wanting.

In the early 20th century, when the international community was moving towards codifying the various aspects of international law, piracy was also one of the many subjects considered worthy of regulation[2]. However, at this point in time, piracy had been virtually unheard of for over half a century. The international community, therefore, considered piracy a relic of the bygone era. Perhaps, it was thought inconceivable that piracy could occur in an era of steel hulled merchant ships and warships with superior firepower and steam powered propulsion.

As a result of the lack of perceived threat of piracy by the international community, the issue was not debated or discussed adequately. The states broadly agreed that piracy was an international crime and that all states were granted universal jurisdiction to prosecute the pirates.[3] In 1932, the Harvard Law School undertook a voluntary study into the various legal aspects of piracy. This study, known as the 'Harvard Draft' was published in 1932 as a draft convention and contained 19 articles of piracy with associated commentary.

The Harvard Draft defined piracy in Article 3 as follows:

Piracy is any of the following acts, committed in a place not within the territorial jurisdiction of any state:

- An act of violence or of depredation committed with intent to rob, rape, wound, enslave, imprison or kill a person or with intent to steal or destroy property, for private ends without bona fide purpose of asserting a claim of right, provided that the act is connected with an attack on or from the sea or in or from the air. If the act is connected with an attack which starts from on board a ship, either that ship or another ship which is involved must be a pirate ship or a ship without national character.

- Any act of voluntary participation in the operation of a ship with knowledge of facts which make it a pirate ship.
- Any act of instigation or of intentional facilitation of an act described above in this article.

The Harvard draft of 1932 later formed the basis for the work on piracy of the International Law Commission (ILC) for inclusion in the Geneva Convention of the High Seas, 1958. The ILC adopted the definition proposed by the Harvard draft, limiting the acts exclusively to high seas and for private ends.

United Nation Conference on the Law of the Sea (UNCLOS) and IMO

In 1978-79 when the topic of piracy came up for discussions during the third United Nation Conference on the Law of the Sea (UNCLOS) piracy had been virtually non-existent for nearly a century. Therefore, the old definition of the Geneva Convention of the High Seas was adopted by the Third UNCLOS, 1982 under Article 101[4] without much ado. The UNCLOS has eight articles devoted to piracy i.e. 100 to 107 (the articles are reproduced at Annexure I).

Piracy was brought to the notice of IMO in 1983 when Sweden asked the Maritime Safety Committee (MSC) to consider an alarming situation off the coast of West Africa where ships were being attacked at anchor at night by armed robbers moving in high-speed boats[5]. Subsequently, an IMO resolution was passed urging all states to accord highest priority to suppress acts of piracy and armed attacks on ships in or adjacent to their waters. The IMO has since been monitoring all piracy incidents and has issued several resolutions to suppress piracy. It also issues important instructions and guidelines for ship owners, operators, crew, etc for avoiding piracy attacks. The IMO is thus the *de facto* international body dealing with all matters pertaining to piracy.

The definition of piracy under UNCLOS, 1982 served the purpose of providing an acceptable definition of piracy under which a state may act to suppress or punish without condemnation from another state for acting out of turn[6]. However, the UNCLOS does not prescribe any punishment for piracy. Today, the definition of piracy under UNCLOS is outdated since, in recent years several attacks on ships were reported in territorial waters of states. As a result, many of the incidents reported do not qualify as pirate attacks. A revised definition of piracy was thus promulgated by the International Maritime Bureau (IMB) as follows:

"... the act of boarding any vessel with an intent to commit theft or any other crime, and with an intent or capacity to use force in furtherance of that act."

The two different definitions of IMO and IMB reflect the various priorities of the IMO as an international organisation under the United Nations Organisation (UNO) and the IMB as a commercial organisation under the International Chamber of Commerce (ICC), representing the shipping industry. The differences in definitions often cause confusion about the scale and types of attacks and inhibits the development of policy responses[7]. This was evident in Southeast Asia where the littorals maintained that there were no piracy attacks in the Strait of Malacca since technically the straits were within the territorial waters of the littoral states; even though the number of armed attacks on ships in the region had reached a peak globally. The salient differences are summarised in the table back side:

Salient Differences between IMO and IMB definitions of piracy

IMO	IMB
Piracy must be committed on the high seas or in a place outside the jurisdiction of any state. A criminal attack with weapons on ships within territorial waters is an act of armed robbery and not piracy	Distinctions do not exist between attacks on the high seas and in territorial waters
Piracy necessitates a 'two ship' requirement. Pirates need to use a ship to attack another ship. This excludes mutiny and privateering from acts of piracy.	A ' two ship' requirement is abolished. Attacks from a raft or even from the quay are acts of piracy.
Piracy is committed for private ends. This excludes acts of terrorism and environmental activism.	Piracy may not only be committed for private ends. Attacks on a ship for political or environmental reasons qualify as piracy.
Because pirate attacks have to be committed by the crew or passengers of privately owned vessels, attacks by naval craft fall outside the bounds of piracy.	The acts of government naval craft can be deemed as piracy in certain circumstances.

Source: Graham Gerad Ong-Webb, 'Introduction: Southeast Asian Piracy: Research and Developments,' in Piracy Maritime Terrorism and Securing the Malacca Straits, edited by Graham Ong-Webb (Singapore, Institute of Southeast Asian Studies, 2006), p xiii.

Convention on the Suppression of Unlawful Activities Against the Safety of Maritime Navigation (SUA Convention)

While the UNCLOS provided a universally accepted definition of piracy and defined the scope of the jurisdiction of states to tackle piracy, it did not provide the legal basis for action to be taken against persons committing various crimes at sea. This inadequacy was resolved by the Convention on the Suppression of Unlawful Activities Against the Safety of Maritime Navigation (SUA Convention, also known as the Rome Convention) which was adopted by the IMO in 1986. The text of the SUA Convention of 1988 is at Annexure 2.

The origin of the SUA Convention lies in the well-known case of the hijacking - by four members of the Palestine Liberation Organisation (PLO) - of the Italian cruise line, SS *Achille Lauro* with 400 passengers, outside the territorial waters of Egypt on October 07, 1985[8]. This incident was in retaliation to the October 01, 1985 Israeli raid on PLO headquarters. The hijacker held the Italian crew and passengers from various countries as hostage and threatened to kill them unless fifty Palestinian prisoners held in Israel were released. The hijackers ordered the vessel to proceed first to Syria and later to Cyprus where they were refused port entry. The vessel then returned within fifteen miles of Port Said, when Egyptian authorities negotiated a safe passage for them in return for the release of the ship and hostages. US Navy fighter planes later intercepted the Egyptian aircraft carrying the hijackers and forced it to land at an Italian military base. The US sought the extradition of the hijackers and issued warrants of arrest, charging them with acts of piracy and seizing control of the ship without authority.

The *Achille Lauro* incident highlighted the inadequacy of the UNCLOS since the incident did not technically qualify as an act of piracy. Firstly, it did not involve two ships as defined under Article 101 nor were the actions of the terrorists for meeting 'private ends.' Therefore, on the suggestion of Austria, Egypt and Italy, directly as a sequel to the *Achille Lauro* case, the UN General Assembly, *inter alia*, requested the IMO to address this anomaly. The IMO Council, in turn established an *ad hoc* committee to prepare a draft convention to prohibit a broad range of acts of violence directed against ships or shipping. Thus, the Suppression of Unlawful Activities Against the Safety of Maritime Navigation Convention was adopted on March 10, 1988 by consensus and an additional protocol adopted, extended the provisions of the convention to fixed platforms at sea on the continental shelf. Both the convention and protocol entered into force on March 01, 1992[9].

The SUA Convention (reproduced at Annexure II) under Article 3 lists seven offenses which the contracting governments are obliged to prosecute or extradite the offenders. These offenses are as follows:

- Seizure of a ship by force or threat or intimidation.
- Acts of violence against person onboard a ship if that act is likely to endanger the safe navigation of a ship.
- Destroying a ship or causing damage to a ship or its cargo which is likely to endanger the safe navigation of a ship.
- Placing a device that is likely to destroy or damage maritime navigational facilities or interfere with their operation.
- Injure or kill any person in connection with the commission or attempts to commit the above offences.

A protocol adopted by IMO simultaneously extends the requirements of the convention to fixed platforms located on the continental shelf. Both the SUA Convention and the Protocol came into force on March 01, 1992. Subsequently, in 2005, Articles 1 to 16 of the convention were revised by the 2005 Protocol. The salient changes brought about by the 2005 Protocol are as follows[10]:

- A substantial broadening of the ambit of offenses under Article 3 was introduced.
- Introduction of provisions in Article 8 to allow for boarding of vessels suspected of being involved in terrorist activities.
- Inclusion of new offences in Article 5 of the Protocol, recognizing the need to include offences against security of navigation alongside the existing offences against the safety of navigation.
- Obligation on contracting governments either to extradite or prosecute alleged offenders.
- Inclusion of important safeguards, not endangering the safety of life at sea, ensuring that all persons onboard are treated in a manner which preserves human dignity and is in keeping with human rights law, taking due account of safety and security of the ship and its cargo, ensuring that measures taken are environmentally sound and making reasonable efforts to avoid a ship being unduly detained or delayed.

Indian Laws dealing with Piracy and Maritime Crimes

UNCLOS: India signed the UNCLOS in December 1982 and later ratified it in June 1995. However, India is yet to enact the domestic laws required to implement the provisions contained in the UNCLOS. Thus, the Indian Penal Code dealing with various crimes does not *per se* address the issues of maritime piracy.

SUA Convention: India ratified both the SUA Convention and Protocol in 2002. Under the SUA convention, contracting states are encouraged to enact specific laws under the Convention. Consequently, in 2005 the Indian Parliament enacted a legislation under the SUA Convention titled; The Weapons of Mass Destruction and Their Delivery System Act, to deal with acts of terrorism that threaten the security of passengers and crew and safety of ships. India thus emerged as the first few states to enact a law under the SUA Convention.

Admiralty Courts of India

The Admiralty jurisprudence system was brought by the Britishers and courts for administering maritime law were established in most British colonies of the world. These Admiralty courts exercised their powers until they were replaced by local legislation. Accordingly, the Indian Admiralty Act was first enacted in 1861 and High Courts were established at Madras, Bombay and Calcutta. There were subsequent acts enacted in 1873, 1920 and 1925. The 1925 Act called Consolidation Act was passed to consolidate all previous acts and vested the Admiralty Jurisdiction in all divisions of the High Court.

Since independence, there has been no Act in India dealing with Admiralty jurisdiction and thus the High Courts of Chennai, Mumbai and Kolkata continue to exercise the Admiralty jurisdiction *mutatis mutandis* (a legal term which means 'by changing those things which need to be changed' or more simply ' the necessary changes having been made') under Article 372 of the Indian Constitution.

The Case of the *Alondra Rainbow*

The Admiralty Act was used, probably for the first time in recent years when in October 1999, the Indian Navy and Coast Guard in a joint operation apprehended the Japanese vessel MV *Alondra Rainbow* and arrested the Indonesian pirates onboard. Even though India had ratified the UNCLOS in 1995, it had not been incorporated into its legislation. Further, in 1999 India had not signed the 1988 SUA Convention and its Protocol (India signed and ratified the SUA Convention in 2002). Thus, the 15 Indonesian pirates arrested in a joint operation by the Indian Navy and Coast Guard were handed over to Mumbai police who charged them on 11 counts under the Indian Penal Code 1860, Indian Passport Act of 1967, Foreigners Act of 1946, the Indian Arms Act of 1950 and charged them for committing piracy under the Admiralty Offences (Colonial) Act, 1849[11]. The trial of the pirates was completed successfully on February 25, 2004 and all pirates were sentenced to seven years of rigorous imprisonment. One pirate died before the trail concluded (for a complete narrative of the incident see Chapter 6).

Modern Challenges to the Current International Legal Framework on Piracy

The extant legal framework on maritime piracy is considered to provide sufficient basis for prosecution of pirates; however, the emergence of piracy in the Gulf of Aden has posed fresh challenges in prosecution of Somali pirates. These challenges are mainly administrative and logistical in nature; imposing a certain economic burden on the prosecuting state.

The seizure of a pirate ship or aircraft and prosecution of pirates is addressed by Article 105 of the UNCLOS as follows:

Article105 - Seizure of a pirate ship or aircraft

On the high seas, or in any other place outside the jurisdiction of any State, every State may seize a pirate ship or aircraft, or a ship or aircraft taken by piracy and under the control of pirates, and arrest the persons and seize the property on board. The courts of the State which carried out the seizure may decide upon the penalties to be imposed, and may also determine the action to be taken with regard to the ships, aircraft or property, subject to the rights of third parties acting in good faith.

The above implies that the pirates arrested at sea should be prosecuted in the national courts of the Flag state of the warship that seized them. Thus, this poses a huge logistical challenge of transporting pirates to the Flag state to stand trial. In 2006, these difficulties caused the United States to provide temporary custody for Somali pirates on board USN warships for months at a time [12]. Even in 2009, it was reported that over 60% of the pirates captured during Operation Atlanta were released for want of proper detention and trial facilities[13]. Thus, many navies have found it more convenient to hand over the arrested pirates or Persons Under Control (PUCs) to Kenya for trials. The EU, UK and USA have signed a memorandum of understanding for prosecution of captured pirates with Kenya under the UN Resolution 1897 of November 2009.[14] However, there is a limit on the capacity of Kenyan prisons. Kenya (as on April 2010) held more than 100 PUCs and had announced that it would not accept any more Somali pirates[15].

Consequently, on April 06, 2010 Russia introduced a draft resolution on Somali piracy in

Fig. 3.1 A Prison in Kenya overflowing with arrested Pirates

the Security Council. The draft recommends possible options such as special domestic chambers, regional tribunal or an international tribunal for ensuring prosecution and incarceration of pirates captured off the coast of Somalia[16]. A Contact Group on Piracy off the Coast off Somalia (chaired by Denmark), established under UN Resolution 1851/ 2009 and the EU are also concurrently studying various judicial issues[17]. Some options currently being studied are as follows[18]:

- ***Specialised Court:*** Setting up of a specialised court to try acts of piracy as defined under the law of the sea, backed by the international community. While the specialised court will conform to international standards of human rights, its procedural rules could be suitably modified or relaxed to take into account operational constraints, specific to contributing navies viz rules regarding presentation of evidence, use of video conferencing for witnesses, etc. These courts could be established in neighbouring countries such as Kenya or even Seychelles.
- ***Somali Court:*** A court established in Somalia alongside the UNODC – the UNODC is currently

running EU financed programmes to construct prisons in Bosaso and Gardo in Somalia – to try Somali pirates.

- ***Relocated Court:*** Pending normalisation of security conditions in Somalia a court could be relocated in another state - accessible by sea – resting on an agreement between Somali authorities and the host state or an international organisation.

Role of India

India is conspicuous by its absence in the ongoing international debate seeking a formal resolution to the challenges of prosecuting Somali pirates. This debate is currently dominated by the EU. It is opined that, India as a growing maritime power should also play a role in the evolving legal framework. Perhaps, India as one of the largest providers of manpower to the shipping industry and thus a major victim of piracy in the Gulf of Aden could additionally take up this issue in the UN General Assembly for discussions with other developing maritime states. This would help to evolve a general consensus among the other states, particularly in the IOR.

Conclusion

Today, piracy is accepted by all countries as a crime of universal jurisdiction and in accordance with the UNCLOS, all states have the right and responsibility to prosecute pirates arrested by their authorised agencies i.e. navy or coast guard. The implementation of this legal framework depends on each state's domestic laws, capacity of the law enforcement agency and the political will to bring the pirates to trial. With the incorporation of the SUA convention in the Indian domestic law and the experience of the Alondra Rainbow, the Indian judicial system is well equipped to handle cases of piracy. Moreover, by deploying the Indian navy ships on anti-piracy patrols in the Gulf of Aden, the government of India has also amply demonstrated its political resolve to fight piracy in the Indian Ocean.

Further, the new Maritime Agenda 2010-20 (released by the Indian Government in January 2011) seeks to frame a new legislation to combat piracy.

The challenges being faced by security agencies in prosecution of the Somali pirates are currently being debated at the UN Security Council, the Contact Group on Piracy off the Coast off Somalia (chaired by Denmark) and the EU. The final objective of the international community, should be to ensure a fair trial and detention of the Somali pirates under conditions which conform to international standards and India as the lead maritime power in the Indian Ocean should play a greater role in the evolving legal framework.

Endnotes

1. Secretary-General, SG/SM/12891, GA/10941 dated May 14, 2010. www.un.org. Accessed on June 20, 2010.
2. Penny Campbell. A Modern History of the International Legal Definition of Piracy. Piracy and Maritime Crimes; Historical and Modern Case Studies. Naval War College Press, New Port, Rhode Island, USA. ISBN No: 978-1-884733-65-9.
3. Ibid.
4. OP Sharma. Piracy at Sea; Legal Aspects. *Journal of Indian Ocean Studies*, Volume 7, Nos 2 and 3, March 2000.
5. Ibid.
6. Ibid. Note 1.

7. Bruce A Elleman, Andrew Forbes and David Rosenberg . Piracy and Maritime Crime. Historical and Modern Case Studies.. Naval War College, Newport Rhode Island, USA.
8. OP Sharma .The International Law of the Sea, India and the UN Convention of 1982. p. 226. OUP, 2009.
9. Ibid.p 225.
10. Ibid. p 227.
11. Ibid.
12. Ibid.
13. Interview with Fredrick Grare, Delegation de Affaires Stratigue (DSA), France.
14. Ibid.
15. Security Council Report on Somalia Piracy dated April 20, 2010.
16. Security Council Update Report. No 3, April 20, 2010.
17. Ibid.
18. Ibid. Note 8.

Chapter – IV

Piracy in the Gulf of Aden

"The area (Gulf of Aden and the Arabian Sea) is enormous and we just do not have enough assets to cover every place in the Indian Ocean"

—Admiral Mark Fitzgerald, USN[1]

***

Piracy in the Gulf of Aden is the manifestation of a greater problem being faced by Somalia; existing without a central and effective government since the overthrow of the authoritarian regime of Said Barre in January 1991.[2] The UN Mission withdrew in 1995 leaving Somalia a classic failed state with factional violence, lawlessness, poverty and famine. Today, Somalia carries the dubious distinction of being the longest-running instance of a failed state in the post-colonial history[3]. The lack of security ashore has spilled into the maritime domain where there is a lack of regional maritime capacity and no credible indigenous maritime forces[4]. Currently, Somalia exists in three parts, independent Somaliland in the Northwest, autonomous region of Puntland in the Northeast and the Southern region dominated by the terrorist outfit Al Shabab, an affiliate of the Al Qaeda[5].

As a result, the decade following the collapse of the Somali government saw extensive poaching activities by Asian and European fishing fleets in the Somali Exclusive Economic Zone (EEZ). There were also reports of toxic waste being dumped in the Somali waters, which subsequently washed ashore. According to a lesser-known study by the UNO, Somalia was losing $ 300 million annually due to poaching in its EEZ[6]. All this led to the emergence of self-styled armed protection groups such as the Somali National Volunteer Coast Guard and the Puntland Coast Guard; aimed at combating poaching and dumping of toxic waste.

The self styled coast guard groups took it upon them to attack illegal poachers. Soon, they graduated on to attacking private yachts transiting the Somali EEZ. However, the Somali pirates made global headlines for the first time when on November 05, 2005, they attempted to hijack the American cruise liner *Seabourn Spirit* approximately 75 nautical miles off the coast of Somalia. This unsuccessful attack triggered a wave of piracy attacks along the Somali coast. Subsequently, Somali pirates made headlines in India when in February 2006, they hijacked an Indian dhow named *Bhakti Sagar* (registered in Porbandar) whilst on passage to Kisamayu. 25 Indian crew members were held hostage till a large undisclosed amount was paid as ransom by the owners[7] (discussed in Chapter 7).

In 2006, there were 22 incidents of attacks on ships by Somali pirates. The numbers have since increased rapidly; more than doubling with each passing year; from 51 in 2007 to 111 in 2008 and 217 in 2009 and 2010. While the number of attacks has really not increased - thanks to ships adopting the Best Management Practices (BMP-3)[8] promulgated by the UK Maritime Trade Office - the range and audacity of attacks by Somali pirates has increased significantly in recent months. The first instance of a long range hijacking was on March 23, 2010, when a Turkish owned vessel, MV *Frigia*, a bulk carrier with a crew of 21 on board, was hijacked 1350 nautical miles from Mogadishu. More recently, on December 5, 2010, six Somali pirates hijacked the Bangladeshi flagged MV *Jahan Moni* some 67 nautical miles off India's Lakshadweep islands. The map below shows the expanding area of operations of the Somali pirates.

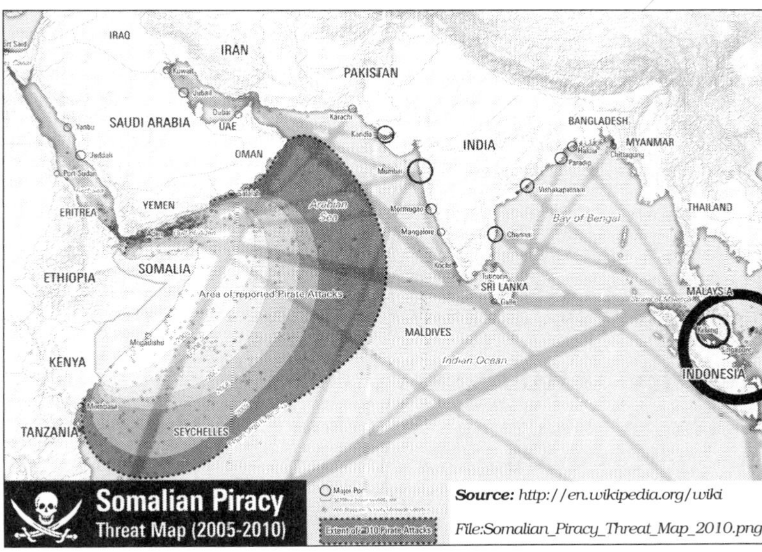

Source: *http://en.wikipedia.org/wiki File:Somalian_Piracy_Threat_Map_2010.png*

In mid 2009, with the arrival of the Second Standing NATO Maritime Group 2 (SNMG2) the number of warships on anti-piracy patrols in the Gulf of Aden had reached a record number of about 25 ships on patrol. To this day almost all the G20 countries are represented in the region including the multinational Task Force 151, European Union Naval Force, NATO and several other naval ships from China, Russia, India, Iran, Japan, South Korea, etc on independent patrol. However, this did not deter the Somali pirates and in 2009 the number of piracy attacks stood at 217; compared to 111 in 2008. Piracy had more than doubled during the period that a record number of warships were on patrol!

It is estimated that the deployment of a frigate sized ship cost approximately $ 50,000 each day at sea[9]. A recent study by the London based think tank, One Earth Future Foundation concluded that about $ 2 Billion is spent on military operations in the region each year. Thus, the questions that arise are; how much longer will the naval patrols need to be sustained in the Gulf of Aden? Are naval anti-piracy patrols the only solution to maintaining security in the shipping lanes? What should be the role of the shipping industry? This chapter seeks to answer these questions. It examines the challenges faced by naval anti-piracy patrols and highlights the various trends in piracy.

Security Initiatives in the Gulf of Aden

The multinational Task Force 150 deployed in the North Arabian Sea since 2003 under the Coalition Maritime Campaign Plan (CMCP) formed the first naval effort to combat piracy. Subsequently, when piracy had reached alarming levels, the UN Security Council adopted Resolution 1816 in June 2008, authorising nations to deploy warships for counter-piracy operations in Somali territorial waters. This was followed by Resolution 1838 in October 2008 urging all maritime states to dispatch naval units to fight piracy, off the Horn of Africa. Presently the key ongoing security initiatives aimed at combating piracy are enumerated in the following paragraphs.

CTF 151: The Coalition Task Force 151 under the United States Fifth Fleet headquarters in Manama, Bahrain was established in January 2009 with a clear mandate to combat piracy in the Gulf of Aden. It comprises of countries engaged in the Coalition Maritime Force (CMF) in the North Arabian Sea region and includes Australia, Bahrain, Pakistan, ROK, Singapore. Turkey, UK and USA. A Maritime Liaison Office (MARLO) facilitates the exchange of information between the United States Navy, Combined Maritime Forces, and the commercial maritime community in the Middle East. The MARLO also monitors the movement of traffic through the IRTC. Presently, two to six ships and a maritime Patrol Aircraft are deployed in the region.

The formation of the CTF 151 in 2009 led to a debate on the issue of India's participation in the multinational patrols. Traditionally, since independence the Indian armed forces have never served under a foreign flag and therefore the government decided to stay out of the multination task force, choosing to deploy Indian naval warships on independent patrols. In the words of Admiral (Retired) Arun Prakash, former naval chief, the time has come for the Indian navy to push for a regional task force under the aegis of the Indian Ocean Naval Symposium (IONS) and invite the other extra regional powers to participate.

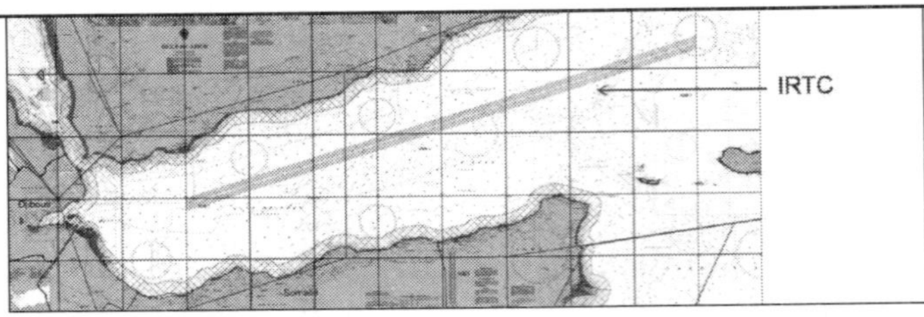

Source: http://asianyachting.com/news/PirateCorridor.htm

Fig. 4.2 IRTC in the Gulf of Aden

International Recommended Transit Corridor (IRTC): The US Navy Central Command (CENTCOM) established the IRTC; a 560 nm long security corridor formerly known as the Maritime Security Patrol Area (MSPA) in the Gulf of Aden on August 22, 2008. This area is currently patrolled by the coalition forces, NATO and EU[10]. The coalition forces have since repulsed several attacks by Somali pirates, even though some successful hijacking have taken place within the IRTC.

SHADE (Shared Awareness and Deconfliction): A series of regular meetings of the naval representatives from China, India, Russia and others from EU and the CMF participating in the anti-piracy patrols held under the US Central Command (CENTCOM) have come to be known as SHADE. The aim of SHADE is to share information and streamline the tactical operating procedures. The SHADE is currently co-chaired by EU and CMF.

Operation 'Ocean Shield' by NATO: A Standing NATO Maritime Group (SNMG) has been deployed in the region to allow World Food Organisation to fulfill its mission of providing humanitarian aid to Somalia under the UN World Food Programme. The operation has been codenamed 'Ocean Shield'. The SNMG comprises of about three to eight ships from

UK, Spain, Italy, Portugal, Turkey, USA, Canada, Denmark, and Greece.

EU Naval Force (EUNAVFOR): A convoy escort system codenamed Operation 'Atlanta' is being maintained by anything between five to fourteen ships of the 27 nation European Union. About three to five Maritime Patrol Aircraft are also employed for surveillance in the region. The main missions of the EU Naval Force are:

- The protection of United Nations World Food Programme Shipping delivering humanitarian food aid to Somalia;
- The protection of merchant vessels transiting through the Gulf of Aden or in proximity to Somalia;
- The deterrence and repression of acts of piracy and armed robbery off the Somali coast.

The following EU Member States have committed assets to the EUNAVFOR - Greece, France, Belgium, Sweden, Netherlands, Norway, Germany, Italy, Spain and UK. The EU has also established the Maritime Security Centre, Horn of Africa or MSC (HoA) in partnership with the industry to improve coordination between commercial shipping and international military forces in the region[11].

Maritime Security Centre (Horn of Africa): The MSC (HoA) is a Coordination Centre, tasked to safeguard merchant shipping operating in the region by preventing and deterring acts of piracy in the Gulf of Aden, off the Horn of Africa and in the Somali Basin. The MSC HoA plays the lead role in monitoring all vessels transiting through the Gulf of Aden and also communicates alerts to ships in the region through an interactive website. The MSC HoA is assisted by the UK Maritime Trade Office in Dubai.

UN Resolution 1816/ 2008: In June 2008 the UN Security Council passed this resolution to give foreign warships the right to enter Somali waters for the purposes of repressing acts of piracy and armed robbery at sea by all necessary means. However, entry into Somali water is permitted with the consent of the Somali Transitional Federal Government (STFG) based on a bilateral agreement.

UN Resolution 1851/ 2009: This resolution adopted in January, 2009 established the Contact Group on Piracy off the Coast of Somalia. Today its membership has grown from 30 countries to more than 50. Six International organisations viz The African Union, the Arab League, EU, IMO, NATO and the UN Secretariat are members. The contact group has a rotating Chairmanship and has four working groups as below:

- Military and operational coordination, information sharing and capacity building – Chaired by UK.
- Judicial issues – Chaired by Denmark.
- Strengthening shipping self awareness and other capacities – Chaired by USA.
- Public Information – Chaired by Egypt.

Independent Anti-piracy Patrols: Several counties have deployed their navies on independent patrols for safety of their merchant ships. These include Japan, China, Iran, Russia, India, South Korea and Saudi Arabia.

Djibouti Code of Conduct: The Djibouti Code of Conduct - inspired by the 2004 Regional Co-Operation Agreement on Combating Piracy and Armed Robbery against Ships (ReCAAP) in Asia - for the repression of piracy and armed robbery against ships in the Western Indian Ocean and

Gulf of Aden came into force from January 29, 2009. It was signed in Djibouti by nine countries of the region; Djibouti, Ethiopia, Kenya, Somalia (TFG), Yemen, Madagascar, Maldives, Seychelles and Tanzania. The Code of Conduct is open for signature by 21 countries in the region. The signatories of the Djibouti Code of Conduct have agreed to establishment of Piracy Information Exchange Centres at Kenya, Tanzania and Yemen, and a regional training centre in Djibouti.

The response of the international community to piracy has been unprecedented. Never before has such a large multinational naval force participated in ensuring security of the seas. Perhaps, this gives the first indications of how a multi-polar world might look like.[12] In such a scenario, there is no room for regional sensitivities; as the Arab states learnt.

GCC Navies

Alarmed by the drop in Suez Canal toll taxes (According to the study by the One Earth Future Foundation Egypt's losses are estimated at $ 642 Million each year[13]) due to ships following the longer yet safer Cape of Good Hope route, a meeting of the representatives of the GCC members was held at the behest of Egypt at Riyadh on June 29, 2009 to discuss the role of the GCC in combating piracy in the Gulf of Aden. This included six member of the GCC viz Bahrain, Kuwait, Oman, Qatar, Saudi Arabia and the United Arab Emirates and the Arab Red Sea littoral countries (Djibouti, Egypt, Jordan, Sudan and Yemen) In a joint statement, it was declared that it is the responsibility of the littoral countries to maintain the security of the Red Sea and combat piracy. The meeting suggested the formation of an Arab naval taskforce against piracy in tune with the international laws and the resolutions of the United Nations Security Council for safeguarding the oil and LNG tankers passing through the Red Sea against the risks of piracy.[14]

However, realising the growing threat of maritime terrorist attacks on their essential infrastructure, including oil facilities, power plants, desalination plants, etc., the Gulf States are now coordinating their efforts with multinational forces for a comprehensive security regime.

Challenges

Despite the fact that the naval patrols have succeeded in destroying a large number of 'mother boats' used by the Somali pirates and also captured a significant quantity of arms and equipment used by the pirates, the number of successful hijackings by Somali pirates remains at unacceptably high levels; 42 in 2008 and 47 in 2009 and 49 in 2010. The attacks by Somali pirates have only increased in audacity and range in recent months with some ships being hijacked in the Red Sea and even close to the West coast of India. The main factors that hamper warship efforts at countering piracy in the Gulf of Aden are enumerated in the succeeding paragraphs.

Lack of Investments in Ship Security: One of the key stakeholders in ensuring maritime security is the shipping industry. The lack of propensity on part of the shipping sector to invest in security stems from the fact that most ships involve multiple stakeholders and thus there is a tendency to 'pass the buck'. Several USA and British Private Security Companies (PSC) offer security solutions for ships transiting the Gulf of Aden. However, these services are expensive; licensed security guards could typically costs about $ 80,000[15]. The Yemini Navy also provides security in association with a UK PSC for $ 55,000 per trip through the Gulf of Aden[16]. However, a majority of the shipping companies are reluctant to invest in expensive security solutions. This can be partly attributed to the impact global recession, which has led to reduced freight earning by shipping companies who in turn are forced to cut down their operating expenses.

An analysis of various incidents reveals several attempts at hijacking have been successfully thwarted due to timely alarm being raised by the target ship or employment of basic security measures. In fact, until 2009 no ship which deployed electric guardrails or barbed wire fencing was hijacked. In 2010, out of a total number of 16 cases wherein the crew members had sought shelter in a citadel, none could be hijacked[17]. On the other hand, in many cases ships which did not adopt even basic security measures or comply with BMP3 guidelines were captured with ease. Once the pirates are onboard the situation is difficult to salvage and even warships with skilled marine commandoes onboard can do little to help. The onboard security options before the merchant ships can be broadly divided into active and passive measures as follows:-

- ***Active Measures:*** These include onboard armed guards or Sea Marshalls, self defence devices such as the Long Range Acoustic Device (LRAD), the recently developed Green Laser gun which can causes temporary blindness, etc.
- ***Passive Measures:*** These measures include high speeds by ships, evasive manoeuvring, ship wide alarm and surveillance devices, anti-boarding

devices such as electric fencing, armoured doors, water cannons, etc. Most of such measures are listed in the BMP 3 guidelines.

It is evident that ships fitted with security devices are better equipped to detect potential attacks in good time and alert security agencies. Lack of such systems reduces the effectiveness of naval patrols. Yet, most shipping companies are loathe to invest in security. Perhaps, a certain basic security system could be considered as a mandatory suite for ships. This could be on the lines of the ISPS code of 2004 that made fitment of radio/ satellite systems compulsory for ship safety. Moreover, incentives by insurance companies in terms of reduced premiums for ships fitted out with security devices could be a viable option to encourage ships to invest in security systems. An example is the Hart-Swinglehurst – Protected Gulf of Aden Transits, which provide a new war risk product. The insurance cover is provided for financial loss resulting from hijacking and crew protection at a discount of 20-30% since each ship is accompanied by an armed security team[18]. Further, ships could conduct regular anti-piracy drills for the crew on lines of the daily onboard fire fighting drills to improve crew confidence in dealing with pirate attacks.

Lack of Regulations dealing with Armed Protection of Merchant Ships: The extant IMO and IMB regulations do not encourage armed protection of ships since it could lead to increased violence at sea. It is likely that confrontation between armed guards and pirates could lead to secondary/ collateral damage. Presently, the authorisation to carry firearms onboard ships is a decision of the Flag state. However, this would be subject to the laws of the country being visited. In the absence of clearly defined rules of engagement, the use of firearms can pose a serious challenge. This issue has been perceived differently by various states. For example, in the Strait of Malacca region, Singapore is in favour of embarking armed security onboard ships while both Malaysia and Indonesia have strongly opposed this move and banned ships with armed security from entering their territorial waters.

Notwithstanding the controversy regarding use of firearms, there have been many success stories of ships effectively thwarting pirate attacks. In 2009, following the capture of the USA Flagged vessel MV *Maersk Albama*, the USA government advised all US Flagged vessels to carry armed security and soon thereafter, the MV *Maersk Albama* successfully fired and defended itself from pirates when attacked for the second time in November 2009. The US government's decision to encourage carriage of firearms onboard merchant ships follows the recent executive order passed by President Obama declaring piracy as a threat to national security of the USA and forbidding material or financial assistance (read ransom) to pirates[19]. It is believed that a few of the Flag of Convenience states are also actively considering following suit, since under Article 94 of the UNCLOS, the Flag states are responsible for security of the ship. It is reported that German shipping companies are now opting for registration under Flags of Convenience since German law does not permit carriage of firearms onboard merchant ships.

The use of private security for transportation systems on land is not a new practice. Consider the example for moving cash (say a few million dollars) from a bank to another location in the city. Today, the use of an armoured vehicle with a GPS tracking system and well-trained and armed guards is the norm rather than an exception. In stark comparison, a typical merchant ship loaded with billions of dollars worth of cargo would be manned by a skeleton crew of 10-15 unarmed people. Security for shipping hitherto, was not accorded importance since the high seas were considered desolate areas. This is no longer true as the Somali pirates - equipped with medium sized trawlers (mother boats), GPS and radio sets – have demonstrated by hijacking ships closer to India than Somalia!

Thus, the use of private security onboard ships is imperative. However, the use of weapons will have to be regulated by the IMO on similar lines as the ISPS Code, which makes it mandatory for merchant ships to be equipped with radio/ satellite equipment for safety at sea.

Inadequacy of Extant International Laws for Prosecution of Pirates: The most difficult challenge faced by warships on anti-piracy is that of prosecution of persons under control (PUCs). Pirates once detained become 'persons under control.' International law requires that the pirates be tried by the courts of the Flag state of the warship, which apprehended the pirates or carried out the seizure. This poses a serious logistics challenge of transporting the captured pirates to the Flag State to stand trial (this issue has been discussed in detail in Chapter 3).

The lack of proper judicial mechanism is hugely counterproductive to the efforts of the warships in the region. Apprehended pirates go scot free only to return to piracy, with more experience.

Modus Operandi of Somali Pirate Groups[21]

Somali pirate groups operate out of well organised and established camps along the coastline. The coastal town of Eyl in Puntland is considered to be the hub of pirates in the Somali region. Hobyo, Harradheere and Kismayo in Southern Somalia are other important coastal locations for launching attacks. A picture of one such unidentified camp is below:

One of the best trained, disciplined and armed Somali pirate group called "Somali Marines" is known to operate out of Harardheere. This group

Source: *UKMTO*

Fig. 4.3 An Unidentified Pirate Camp in Somalia.

is also known for a proper command and control structure, probably due to the fact that the it has in its cadres ex Somali naval 'Captains' and even 'Admirals' who got their training in the 1980s (some of whom even attended naval academies in the former Soviet Union and who still speak some Russian)[22]. The hijacking of the T72 laden MV Faina and the MV M. Sirius Star (The largest ship to be hijacked) are believed to have been engineered by the Somali Marines of Harardheere.

Given that Haradheere is actually a town and not a port - about 20 Kilometres inland - without a proper harbor, the hijacked vessels are anchored off Hobyo and Eyl – probably in partnership with pirates groups based there. Based on these facts, it is suspected that the Somali Marines operating out of Harardheere are the main long distance hijackers among all the Somali pirate groups, and that they are the one responsible for the expansion of piracy into the waters of the Eastern Arabian Sea, the Maldives, Lakshadweep and Seychelles and the Red Sea.

The pirates carry out attacks using small fast Skiffs which are approximately 23 feet long fiberglass hulled boats fitted out with outboard motor engines. These Skiffs are towed out to sea using a medium sized fishing trawlers or 'Mother Ships;' a majority being captured from Southeast Asian fishermen who fish in the region for Tuna. Pirates use typically two or three skiffs with four

Source: *UKMTO*

Fig. 4.4 Pirates in a Skiff.

to six men posing as fishermen, until the attack begins. The pirates armed with AK 47 assault rifles and RPGs fire at the bridge to intimidate the crew and master. They then board the vessels with extended ladders attached at the end of a sturdy line which has a grappling hook at the other end. Once onboard the pirates head for the bridge to take over control of the ship.

A worrying development in recent weeks has been the use of large captured vessels for launching attacks on other ships. On January 12, 2011, Somali pirates boarded a general cargo vessel some 270 miles Northeast of Socotra Island. The attack was launched from a previously-captured fishing vessel being used as a mother ship.With time it is likely that the Somali pirate groups could evolve into organised groups operating from hijacked merchant ships with the capability to operate in the busy sea lanes of the Indian Ocean region for several days, masquerading as innocent merchant vessels and targeting unsuspecting ships.

Terro-Piracy: The gravest risk of piracy is the threat of terrorist groups linking up with the Somali pirates, hence the term 'Terro-Piracy'. The main terrorist group active in the region is the Al Qaeda Arabian Peninsula or AQAP, an affiliate of the Al Qaeda, operating out of Yemen. In October 2010 the AQAP had claimed responsibility for sending two parcel bombs via UPS and FedEx. The explosives were intercepted in Dubai and England, before they could be detonated, after authorities received a tip from Saudi Arabia. In the past the Al Qaeda had demonstrated its capacity to launch maritime terrorist attacks when it struck the USS Cole and the French Tanker MV Limburg in Aden in 1998 and 2000 respectively. It is likely that the pressures of the Global War on terror on land and aviation security could force the Al Qaeda to move to sea.

The Al Shabab (considered to be another affiliate of the Al Qaeda) is a Somali based terrorist outfit that has recently taken control of several towns in Southern Somalia. According to *Jane's (Intelligence Review)* pirate groups pay a part of their earnings as protection money to the Al Shabab. Clearly, the ransom money is thus routed into terrorist activities.

Source: *UKMTO*

Fig. 4.5 Dent of the Ship side of MV M. Star.

The possibility of pirate groups and the terrorist outfits jointly carrying out maritime terrorist attacks in the future can't be ruled out. The curious case of the MV *M. Star* is an important example. In July 2010 a Japanese oil tanker, MV *M. Star* reported being hit by an unidentified object whilst on passage through the Strait of Hormuz. A crew reported seeing a flash on the horizon shortly before the impact. Luckily the ship survived the blast with minimal damage save for a dent of the ship side (as seen in picture). The ship was subsequently examined by experts from the US Navy in UAE and traces of explosives were found on the ship side. The US Department of Transportation has now revealed that the attack was probably a failed suicide attack by an affiliate of the Al Qaeda.

Trends

Ransom: According to the One Earth Future Foundation study report of December 2010 the ransom collected by Somali pirates in 2009 was estimated at $ 177 million and in 2010 at $ 238 Million. Evidently, a large part of this amount has been ploughed back into business to procure better equipment and weapons. The Somali pirates are now equipped with GPS, automatic rifles, Rocket Propelled grenade launchers and high speed boats! The increased range and audacity of attacks clearly indicates improved tactics and better equipment in the hand of the pirates.

The average ransoms demanded by Somali pirates have increased from $ 100,000 to 200,000 in 2005 to $ 5.4 million in 2009[23]. In November 2010, the highest ransom ever, $ 9.5 Million was paid to secure the release of *Samho Dream*, a South Korean oil tanker. It is also evident that the pirates have realised that the success of the business depends on a 'non violent' method of extraction. The statistics recorded by IMB indicate that the pirates have deliberately abstained from violence against the crew. In 2008, over 800 crew members had been held as hostage; three were killed. In 2009, over 860 crew members had been taken hostage; four were killed.

A piracy incident of September 2008 seems to support this; during the hijacking of the Ukrainian freighter; The *Faina*, off Somalia, the pirate leader admitted via phone to a New York Times reporter that the group wanted "just money.[24]" However, it is opined that with increasingly audacious piracy attacks in high seas, the scale of violence may increase in the future.

Insurance: The rise in ransom demands has been accompanied by an increase in insurance premiums. Since 2008, the insurance surcharge for ships transiting the Gulf of Aden has increase 300 fold from $ 500 per ship, per voyage to up to $ 150,000 per ship, per voyage in 2010. Accordingly, the shipping companies have increased their freight charges to include the insurance surcharge and also additional risk pay for crew. The Shipping Corporation of India has recently introduced a piracy risk surcharge of $ 40/ TEU on all shipments thorough the Gulf of Aden[25]. This increased freight is passed on to the exporter by the shipping agent. Eventually, the sum is passed on to the final consumers.

Over 24,000 ships transit the Gulf of Aden annually. In 2010, 49 ships were hijacked by Somali pirates and $238 million paid in ransom. The ransom is usually paid by the insurance companies through their agents in cash and the sum is generally undisclosed. Comparatively, the current rates of surcharge ($ 150,000 per ship, per voyage) would have fetched insurance companies anything between $ 1 to 3 Billion. Clearly, even a conservative estimate of the total insurance surcharge paid by the shipping companies is much greater than the total ransom paid by insurers. Thus, the system of ransom has emerged as a lucrative business model with both the insurance companies and the pirates making a neat sum at the expense of the end consumer.

Conclusion

Piracy in the Gulf of Aden, which first made headlines in 2005, is now a well-established industry. The fact that the system of ransom is turning out to be a lucrative business for pirates and insurance companies, sets a dangerous precedence. Clearly, in such a scenario, the interests of the crew are not being addressed as ship-owners are reluctant to invest in ship security and prefer to take their chances at sea. The additional insurance surcharge is passed on the end consumer of the goods with no dues to the ship-owners.

Warship patrols in the Gulf of Aden has reached a record number with a majority of the G20 navies operating in the region. Yet, piracy continues to flourish, at greater ranges. Pirates armed with sophisticated weapons and equipment operate with impunity at great ranges. The high seas are no longer desolate areas where unarmed ships with a handful of men can sail undisturbed. Warships cannot be omnipresent and therefore there is a need for the merchant ships to invest in security. However, this calls for a new regulation to be drafted. Perhaps, this could be done on the lines of the ISPS code implemented in 2004.

The scourge of piracy can only be addressed by collaborative efforts on part of the three main stakeholders ie the shipping industry, the security agencies and the international maritime organisations such as the IMO and ITWF. India as the largest provider of skilled manpower to the maritime sector could play an important role in ensuring participation by all the stakeholders.

Endnotes

1. VOA news.com. Accessed on April 25, 2010.
2. Dr Peter Lehr. The Threat of Piracy and Maritime Terrorism to International Shipping: Developing Effective Measures of Mitigation. TRANSEC Conference, Mumbai. September 2009.
3. Trinanjan Radhakrishnan. Tackling Somali Piracy: Towards a Political Solution. *Maritime Affairs*. Vol. 6 No. 1 Summer Edition 2010.p 142.
4. Dr Thean Potgieter, Stellenbosch University, South Africa and Dr Clive Schofield, ANCORS, University of Wollongong, Australia. Horn of Troubles: Maritime Aspects of Food Security and Law and Order off Somalia. Proceedings from the Indian ocean maritime security symposium, Australian Defence College, Canberra, Australia. 15-17 April 2009.
5. Robert Kaplan, 'Monsoon.' P 304. Random House, New York, 2010.
6. Ibid.
7. Adm (Retd) Arun Prakash. The Menace of Piracy: UN Blue Ensign To The Rescue? NMF Web Commentary; www.maritimeindia.org. Accessed on June 17, 2010.
8. A document prepared by the UKMTO which lays down guidelines for ships to practice in piracy infested waters.
9. Peter Chalk, Laurence Smallman, Nicholas Burger. Countering Piracy in the Modern Era. Notes from a RAND Workshop to Discuss the Best Approaches for Dealing with Piracy in the 21st Century. Published in 2009 by the RAND Corporation.
10. ICC Commercial Crime Services Newsletter dt 26 Aug 08.
11. www.mschoa.eu. Accessed on 26 April 2010.
12. Paper presented by Cmde Retd Ranjit B Rai at the 6th MIMA Conference in June 2009. 'The legal international perspective of the Malacca Straits and

Indian views therein"the US-India-China strategic game plan in the IOR and China's string of pearls.'

13. The Economic Costs of Maritime Piracy. Anna Bowden. One Earth Future Foundation, Working Paper, December 2010.
14. Paul Handley, AFP news report, June 29, 2009 (accessed December 20, 2009).
15. Note xiii ibid. p 15. Also see MARAD,' Economic Impact of Piracy in the Gulf of Aden,' and Emmanuel,'Time to Join the Fight Against Maritime Piracy.'
16. Sam Bateman, "Riding Shotgun; Armed Security Guards onboard Merchant Ships" RSIS Commentary, March 5, 2010.
17. Discussions with Director IMB during the Middle East Maritime Summit 2010 at Abu Dhabi from November 29 to December 01, 2010.
18. Lok Vi Ming and Laura Cheng, "Maritime Insurance Against Pirates: A Shield or a Sword?" Presented at the International Maritime Security Conference 2009, Singapore.
19. *Trade Winds*, 23 April 2010. Volume I Number 16.
20. Peter Chalk, "The Maritime Dimensions of International Security, terrorism, Piracy and Challenges for the United States," RAND Monograph. p. 15.
21. Most of the information in this paragraph is based on the authors interaction with representatives from the UKMTO, MARLO, MSC HoA and others who participated in the Middle East Maritime Summit 2010 at Abu Dhabi from November 29 to December 01, 2010.
22. http://www.fairplay.co.uk (Accessed on January 03, 2011).
23. Note xiii. Ibid. P 9.
24. Cdr John Patch, USN, ""The Overstated Threat." Proceedings, USN Institute, Dec 2008.
25. *Shipmag*, Vol 7, Issue 1. January 2010.

CHAPTER – V

PIRACY IN SOUTH EAST ASIA

"....Subject to the desire of the littoral states, as a major user-state, India would be willing to assist the project in whatever capacity is deemed suitable. India has developed capabilities in various aspects of maritime security and would be most willing to share its expertise with countries of the region."

—*Pranab Mukherjee*[1]

***

The Strait of Malacca in Southeast Asia is the most important strategic chokepoint in the IOR being the shortest route connecting the Indian and Pacific oceans. Over a third of the world's trade is shipped through this shipping route[2]. Historically, since the early 15th century, piracy in the Strait of Malacca has been a lucrative way of life for the various fishing communities along the coast. The geography of the coastline along the narrow strait lends itself suitable for piracy, allowing the pirates to launch surprise attacks on opportune targets and disappear into the cover of numerous small islands, creeks and coves. In the early 15th century, many of the local pirate groups were used by the Sultan of Malacca to maintain control over various islands. In the 18th century, piracy in the region had increased; spurred by the arrival of colonial powers engaged in spice and opium trade between British India and China[3]. Subsequently, in 1830 the British and Dutch naval forces joined hands to combat piracy in the region. By 1870 piracy had almost disappeared from the region.

Piracy re-emerged in the region towards the end of the 20th century when the Asian financial crisis of 1997 resulted in widespread unemployment, poverty and slow economic growth in the region[4]. In such times, the sight of ships; loaded with food supplies enough to feed an entire village for years, going past the narrow straits would probably have been the incentive for the inheritors (known as *Lanun* in the Malay language) of the historically lucrative trade, to return to piracy. By the year 2004, the number of pirate attacks in the region had reached a record high of 157, accounting for more than half of the global total of 329!

The Strait of Malacca was declared as the world's top piracy hotspot by the International Maritime Bureau (IMB) and placed in the war risk zone by Lloyd's War Committee. This resulted in the levy of additional insurance surcharge for ships transiting the Straits. More significantly, the patrols were prompted by the US' plans of involvement in the security of the Straits through the mechanism of the Regional Maritime Security Initiative (RMSI).While Singapore was supportive of the RMSI, both Malaysia and Indonesia were opposed to foreign naval presence. Malaysia and Indonesia were also critical of Indian Navy's role under Operation Sagittarius for escorting US Navy ships through the straits in the aftermath of the 9/11 attacks. The sensitivities of the regional states for their sovereign rights stems from their historical experience of being colonised by the European powers in the 18th century by virtue of being located astride the world's strategic waterways.

When Operation MALSINDO was launched, many critics had forecast that the regional states would be unable to sustain continuous surveillance in the Straits without support from the US or other extra regional navies. The success of the MALSINDO patrols has silenced such critics, with even the Lloyd's War Committee removed the Straits from its high-risk list in August 2006.

Safety and Security Aspects

The regional states have jointly developed a unique mechanism for ensuring safety and security in the Straits. While the safety aspects are addressed in collaboration with the user states and other stakeholders, the security of the Straits is exclusively under the Malacca Strait Security Initiative (MSSI). The MSSI has now evolved into a comprehensive security regime. Piracy in the region appears to be under control (at least for the time being) though the threat of maritime terrorism continues to remain high. The MSSI has proved to be a highly successful model of partnership between regional states in tackling a common threat. It has also helped the regional states in establishing their position with regard to their sovereign rights, albeit at the cost of stretching the naval resources of the littorals to their limits.

Evolving Regional Threat Scenario

While piracy in the Straits has been brought under control, jointly by the four littoral navies, the threat of maritime terrorism remains. Recently, an intelligence report from Singapore warned of a possible terrorist attack on an oil tanker in the straits[5]. In the prevailing scenario, is the MSSI geared to address the future security challenges, when the maritime resources of the littorals have been stretched too far? Is the issue of sovereign rights of the littorals being taken too far at the cost of jeopardising the security of world shipping? These questions can best be answered by the littorals by holistically examining their capabilities and limitations of coordinated patrols. Perhaps, the time has now come for the regional states to explore the option of co-opting the Indian Navy as a regional partner in order to augment their resources.

History of Regional Cooperation

The three regional states "Malaysia, Indonesia and Singapore"have a long history of mutual cooperation with regard to the Straits. All matters pertaining to the Straits have been jointly discussed at ministerial level meetings. Following, the first ministerial meeting held in October 1971, the states issued a joint statement opposing international legal status to the Straits. They maintained that the safety of the Straits would be coordinated solely by the three littoral states.

Several rounds of ministerial meetings were then conducted between the three states in which various regulations such as the Traffic Separation Scheme, rules for deep draught vessels, etc., were promulgated for compliance through the IMO. A group of experts, known as the Tripartite Technical Experts Group (TTEG), subsequently coordinated policy matters.

UN Laws of the Sea Convention

The Straits are governed by Part II of the UNCLOS pertaining to straits used for international navigation. In accordance with the UNCLOS, all commercial and military vessels have the right of transit passage through the Straits and such rights cannot be impeded or suspended. All ships are obliged to follow the various international rules and regulations pertaining to safety of navigation, pollution control, etc., promulgated by the littoral states through the IMO.[6] This implies that the power to adopt a particular regulation rests with the IMO rather than the littoral state.

Article 43 of the UNCLOS, which governs the responsibilities of user states with regard to use of the international straits, says:

'Navigational and safety aids and other improvements and the prevention, reduction and control of pollution

User States and States bordering a strait should by agreement cooperate

(a) in the establishment and maintenance in a strait of necessary navigational and safety aids or other improvements in aid of international navigation; and

(b) for the prevention, reduction and control of pollution from ships.'

Thus, users are obliged to share the burden of maintaining safety and pollution control in the straits with the littorals. Unfortunately, with the exception of Japan, no other user state has contributed towards the cause of the Straits.[7] However, post 9/11, maritime security suddenly became a high priority. A review of the maritime security was undertaken by IMO and several new regulations, such as the ISPS Code, were promulgated.

Following 9/11, the US initiated various steps such as the Container Security Initiative (CSI) and the Proliferation Security Initiative (PSI). Around the same time, the number of piracy attacks on ships increased considerably in the Straits and the US announced its plans for RMSI. All these developments did not go down well with the littoral states and were discussed in the 2005 joint ministerial meeting at Batam.

The 2005 Batam Joint Ministerial Statement

The Foreign Ministers of Indonesia, Malaysia and Singapore met at Batam in August 2005 to discuss matters pertaining to the safety of navigation, environmental protection and maritime security.[8] The Batam joint statement sets out the views of the three littorals on the roles of the littorals, the user states and international agencies, such as the IMO, in enhancing the safety, security and environmental protection in the Straits.

The statement reaffirmed the sovereign rights of the littorals in the Straits and their primary responsibility for safety of navigation, environmental protection and maritime security. It also recognised the importance of engaging with the funnel states. It states that any cooperative measures taken in the Straits must be in conformity with international law and the UNCLOS.

In regard to the roles for user states and others in cooperative arrangements, the Batam statement, mindful of the responsibility and burden of the littoral states and interests of the user states, welcomed assistance of user states, international agencies and the shipping industry in areas of capacity building, training and technology transfer, and other forms of assistance in accordance with the UNCLOS convention.

Key Challenges

The key challenges in securing the straits as identified by the littorals can be categorised into safety and security threats as follows:-

Safety Hazards

Navigational Accidents: An average of over 60,000 ships transit the Straits annually. It has been projected that the annual traffic in the Straits will increase to 100,000 ships by 2020.[9] With increasing density of shipping, the likelihood of navigational accidents, such as collisions, grounding, etc., will increase significantly. The following table indicates the traffic growth in recent years.

Table5.1 Annual Shipping Traffic Transiting the Strait of Malacca by Types of Ships (as reported by Port Klang's Vessel Traffic System 2000-2006)

Type of Ships	2000	2001	2002	2003	2004	2005	2006
VLCC/ULCC	3,163	3,303	3,301	3,487	3,477	3,788	3,851
Crude/Product tankers	13,343	14,276	14,591	15,667	16,403	14,759	14,784
LNG/ LPG	2,962	3,086	3,141	3,277	3,343	3,099	3,297
General Cargo	6,603	6,476	6,065	6,193	6,624	6,340	6,477
Container	18,283	20,101	20,091	19,575	20,187	20,818	22,615
Bulk	4,708	5,370	5,754	6,256	6,531	7,394	8,129
RORO/Car Carrier	1,761	1,764	1,980	2,182	2,440	2,515	2,863
Passenger	3,301	3,151	3,490	3,033	2,838	2,299	2,009
Livestock	70	108	108	80	46	45	51
Tug/Tow	774	610	422	478	568	420	372
Navy	117	155	111	120	130	153	81
Fishing	44	60	38	35	67	34	39
Others	828	854	942	1,951	982	957	1,081
Total	55,957	59,314	60,034	62,334	63,636	62,621	65,649

Source: Marine Department, Peninsular Malaysia[10]

Environmental Pollution: The Straits are the economic lifeline for millions of local people, who earn their living from various activities connected with the waterways. Environmental pollution resulting from thousands of ships transiting the straits can lead to degradation of the coastal zones, such as mangroves, coral reefs, etc.[11] This can adversely affect the economies of the regional states in the long run.

Security Threats

Threats from Transnational crimes, Piracy and Maritime Terrorism: Transnational crimes in the region include a wide spectrum of activities, ranging from illegal fishing, sand mining, drug smuggling, human trafficking, etc., to piracy and hijacking of ships. While piracy in the Straits is currently under control, the threat of maritime terrorism continues to remain high. Two leading terrorist groups"Al Qaeda and the *Jemmah Islamiah* (JI)"are known to be active in the region. As terrorist groups have been facing increasing pressures from security agencies on land, there exists a strong possibility of increased maritime terror attacks by global terror groups working in collaboration with pirates.

Cooperative Mechanism for Safety in the Straits

Following the Batam statement in September 2007, the regional states launched a cooperative mechanism for addressing safety concerns in the Straits. This was based upon Article 43 of UNCLOS.

The cooperative mechanism was the first instance of implementation of Article 43 with regard to an international strait. It consists of three elements–a cooperation forum, aids to navigation fund and specific projects.[12] Under it, the Cooperation Forum is intended to promote dialogue and discussions between the littoral states, user states and other interested stakeholders. The Aids to Navigation Fund is intended to enable user states and other stakeholders to make voluntary contributions to enhance navigational safety and environmental protection by maintaining and replacing aids to navigation, such as lighthouses and buoys. A total of six specific projects have been agreed upon by the littoral states to enhance the safety and environmental protection in the straits. These projects are:[13]

- Removal of wrecks in the Traffic Separation Scheme (TSS);
- Cooperation and capacity building in relation to the protocol on Preparedness, Response and Cooperation in Pollution Incidents by Hazardous and Noxious Substances, 2000 (OPRC-HNS Protocol);
- Demonstration project for placing Class B Automatic Identification System transponders on small ships;
- Setting up tide, current and wind measurement systems;
- Replacement and maintenance of aids to navigation; and
- Replacement of navigational aids damaged in the 2004 *tsunami*.

The response of the user states to the projects has been positive, with the main contributors being Japan, China, Australia, South Korea, the US and India. Encouraged by the response of the user states, the littoral states are working on new projects for enhancing safety and environmental protection.

Evaluation of the Cooperative Mechanism: The cooperative mechanism has been hailed as an historic breakthrough. It allows the littoral states to identify projects necessary to address their safety and environmental concerns in the straits and implement them in collaboration with all stakeholders, including user states, international maritime bodies and even the shipping industry.

The success of the cooperative mechanism, particularly in respect of the special projects, will result in an increased responsibility on part of the stakeholders who have committed to investing huge capital. This is likely to lead to the stakeholders demanding a greater share in the affairs of the Straits. In the long run, the outcome could be different from what has been envisaged by the littorals, with the stakeholders demanding a role in the TTEG and joint ministerial meetings.

Security Arrangements in the Straits

The security concerns of the littorals that include a wide spectrum of transnational crimes, piracy, hijacking and maritime terrorism have been kept out of the purview of the cooperative mechanism. The cooperative mechanism has thus been limited to safety and environmental protection.

Malacca Strait Security Initiative

The Malacca Strait Security Initiative was prompted by the US Navy's move to formally present before the US House of Representatives Armed Forces Committee, the Regional Maritime Security Initiative (RMSI) in March 2004. The RMSI was quickly rejected by the littoral countries, with the Malaysian Deputy Prime Minister, Najib Tun Razak, asserting on April 6, 2004, that the "control of the strait is the sovereign prerogative of Malaysia and Indonesia, and the US military involvement is not welcome." He said US vessels "could use the waterway for their ships, including warships, but to launch operations, they should have the concurrence of Malaysia and Indonesia."

Subsequently, on July 20, 2004, 17 ships of Indonesia, Malaysia and Singapore navies conducted a sail past, before the launch of Operation MALSINDO, the anti-piracy and anti-terrorism patrols in the Strait of Malacca.

While rejecting international participation, the littoral states left open their willingness to accept financing, equipment and training from outside nations. The littoral states were severely criticised for being overly sensitive to their sovereign rights. However, a significant drop in the incidents of piracy was observed within a year of the launch of the patrols.

In September 2005, aerial patrols codenamed "Eyes in the Sky"were introduced to augment surface patrols. In 2006, a multi-million dollar project, partly sponsored by the IMO as well as some shipping companies, was launched for setting up a radar chain along the Straits.

Also, in April 2006, a joint accord was signed between Singapore, Malaysia and Indonesia to formally establish a security regime for the straits, bringing both the surface and aerial patrols under one umbrella. Under the accord, the littorals also agreed to establish a joint coordinating committee to coordinate patrols. Control centres were established at various locations in the participating countries and a mechanism for intelligence sharing was also introduced. Recently, a standard operating procedures manual (SOPs) was introduced.

Thailand was conspicuous by its absence from the accord, ostensibly due to political instability in the country, which led to the overthrow of Prime Minister Thaksin. However, since early 2009, Thailand has become an active participant in the MSSI.

The MSSI has evolved into a comprehensive security regime that includes surface patrols (MALSINDO), aerial patrols (Eyes in the Sky) and a chain of radar stations along the straits (SURPIC). All operations are coordinated by the joint coordination committee, with a network of command and control centres in each participating country and an intelligence sharing mechanism.

Extra Regional Initiatives for Security

Regional Cooperation Agreement On Combating Piracy And Armed Robbery Against Ships (ReCAAP)

The ReCAAP was initiated by Japan in 2004 to promote multilateral anti-piracy cooperation. The agreement came into force in September 2006. Under it, the ASEAN 10 as well as Japan, India, China, Korea, Bangladesh and Sri Lanka have agreed to cooperate in areas related to information sharing, mutual capacity building and combined operations. Indonesia and Malaysia have not yet ratified the agreement, though they have agreed to cooperate on the ground. Under ReCAAP, an information sharing centre (ISC) has been established at Singapore. Broadly, the role of the ISC is to carry out an analysis of various transnational crimes, including piracy, in the region with a view to providing the security agencies with the operational intelligence to combat maritime threats.

CARAT Exercises

Notwithstanding the reluctance of Malaysia and Indonesia in seeking direct foreign participation in

sharing centre in Singapore. Further, India has contributed towards at least two out of the six projects in the cooperative mechanism for the straits. This indicates India's high level of commitment to maintaining security in the straits. Any reticence on part of India is to give due regard to regional sensitivities.[14]

However, the consistent stand by the regional countries"based solely on protecting their sovereign rights"to exclude India and other extra regional partners from actively participating in the security patrols can result in serious shortcoming in the security of the Straits. Moreover, such a stand is not in consonance with the requirements of the situation and the evolving security scenario in the region.

There is an urgent need to augment the resources under MSSI in order to sustain all-round surveillance. During the initial years of the security patrols, the littorals adopted a 'foot on the ground' approach, committing several ships for round-the-clock patrols as well as frequent aerial sorties. It is appreciated that such vigorous patrolling will be difficult to sustain, particularly when the littorals will be required to deploy their navies on anti-piracy patrols elsewhere in the Gulf of Aden, as was recently demonstrated by Malaysia and Singapore. In this regard, it is pertinent to note that Thailand, which had successfully dodged its participation in the MSSI since 2004 (citing political instability), was finally coaxed into joining the patrols in 2009, to contribute to the common cause and also augment capability in the northern sector of the Straits.

However, despite Thailand joining the MSSI, it is unlikely to augment the available resources significantly, given its modest naval capability. In any case, the western approaches to the straits are likely to remain under-patrolled under the MSSI. The need of the hour is a modern all-round surveillance system to provide total maritime domain awareness (MDA) and a capability for rapid response to developing security situations through quick response teams (QRTs), which can be deployed at various points along the straits. These are some areas where assistance can be sought from the Indian Navy.

Areas of Cooperation with Indian Navy

In a model similar to the Gulf of Aden security patrols, it would be prudent for the littorals to engage with their immediate maritime neighbour and a funnel state—India— to augment their resources necessary to combat emerging threats in the region and keep pace with the evolving threat scenario. A spillover of transnational crimes to the West into the Andaman Sea, a trend observed in the Gulf of Aden, will necessarily involve the Indian Navy.

India's Stand

India's stand with regard to participation in the MSSI was made clear stated in June 2006 at Singapore by the then Defence Minister, Pranab Mukherjee, during the Shangri La dialogue. He had said "there is a need to increase and strengthen regional cooperation to enhance maritime security.... We believe that through the coordination of our individual efforts, the security of the sea lanes will be enhanced....Subject to the desire of the littoral states, as a major user-state, India would be willing to assist the project in whatever capacity is deemed suitable. India has developed capabilities in various aspects of maritime security and would be most willing to share its expertise with countries of the region."

India's stand and commitment to regional cooperation to enhance maritime security has remained unchanged since then.

Ongoing Foreign Cooperation Programmes

India has close defence ties with all the littoral countries and has provided them with training assistance as well as technical support in several areas. The Indian Navy has been conducting coordinated patrols with two of the four MSSI participants, viz. Thailand and Indonesia, under bilateral agreements signed in 2005 and 2001 respectively. Moreover, the Indian Navy conducts annual exercises with the Republic of Singapore Navy (RSN). Thus, the Indian Navy has established a high degree of interoperability with almost all the littorals and is thus ideally suited to contribute to the security mechanism. This interoperability exists at various levels, ranging from political compatibility at the highest level to tactical operating procedures at the elementary levels.

Ship Patrols along Western Approaches of the Strait of Malacca

The bilateral patrols with Thailand and Indonesia are currently conducted along the international EEZ boundary line established between the countries. The boundary line roughly runs along the western approaches to the Strait of Malacca, through which the entire shipping traffic, moving in and out of the straits, cuts across. A patrol established along the western approaches by the Indian Navy, either singly or jointly with Indonesia and Thailand, can perfectly seal the Strait of Malacca in a security cordon. It is not important that the mechanism for involving the Indian Navy be framed under the aegis of the MSSI or a unified command. Perhaps, it can be an arrangement wherein both sides operate independently and exchange tactical information to augment each other's overall maritime domain awareness. The scope and periodicity of the patrols can be simply adopted by suitably modifying the existing bilateral arrangements with Thailand and Indonesia.

Aerial Surveillance by UAVs and MR Aircraft

The Indian Navy currently operates Unmanned Aerial Vehicles (UAVs) and several aircraft. These can be operated from the Andaman group of islands; an archipelago of 572 islands. The southern tip of these islands is only 165 km from the Strait of Malacca, separated by the Six Degree Channel. The UAVs, launched from the Andaman Group of Islands and operating within a radius of about 100 km, can be tasked for aerial surveillance of the Western approaches or the funnel region of the straits. The UAV can transmit the data/picture on a real time basis to all the joint coordination centres established under the MSSI. The Singapore Navy has also recently acquired UAVs. These can be used in coordination with Indian UAVs to establish all-round aerial surveillance. This will significantly augment the surveillance capacity of the littorals and ease the task of ship patrols. Further, a system of all-round aerial surveillance in the straits coupled with immediate response from Quick Reaction Teams (QRTs) based along the straits will go a long way in improving the security of the straits.

Shipping Traffic in Funnel Region Heading for the Straits

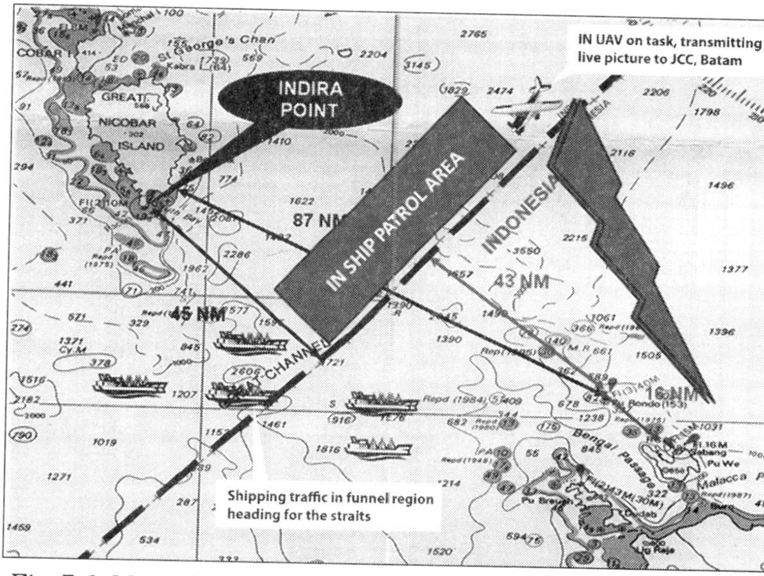

Fig 5.1 Map showing potential areas of surveillance in the Strait of Malacca funnel region by Indian Navy along the EEZ BL with Indonesia

Information Sharing: Virtually, the entire shipping traffic passing through the Straits is routed South of the Indira Point in the Great Nicobar Island. Information about the traffic can be shared with the littorals to provide advance information about the traffic entering the Straits. This will significantly enhance their maritime domain awareness.

Indian Ocean Naval Symposium (IONS): The IONS provides a regional forum through which the Chief of the regional navies (and/or the principal maritime agencies responsible for maritime security) of all the littoral states of the IOR can periodically meet to constructively engage one another. It enables the creation and promotion of regionally relevant mechanisms, events, and activities with a view to arriving at agreed courses of action on trans-national issues, based upon a common understanding of the regional maritime security environment (see Chapter 6).

The IONS is an ideal forum for India to develop a maritime domain partnership in the region with due regard to the sensitivities of the littoral states. Perhaps, the IONS could be used to establish a security construct along with Australia, a key player in the FPDA and an important stakeholder in the safety and security mechanism of the straits. This would go a long way in allaying the fears of the littoral states of extra regional participation.

Conclusion

The Malacca Strait Security Initiative and the cooperative mechanism was jointly launched by Indonesia, Malaysia, Singapore and Thailand in 2004 to counter interference by extra regional powers in the Straits as also to combat transnational crimes and ensure safety of shipping. The MSSI has completed five years of successful operations and helped the littorals to establish and strengthen their sovereign rights in the Straits. Meanwhile, the cooperative mechanism has significantly improved the safety situation in the Straits through greater involvement of the user states, including India and other stakeholders.

However, though the security situation in the region appears to be under control; the littoral navies are overwhelmed with the task of securing the straits. The threat of terrorism in the region shows no signs of abating and in the prevailing situation there is no scope for respite for the security agencies. A single act of maritime terrorism in the Straits can permanently erase the success of the MSSI and also probably, forever change the dynamics of security in the region.

The task of securing the straits in the backdrop of the current security situation demands greater efforts, beyond the combined capacities of the littorals. It can be concluded that the issue of sovereign rights in the Straits has been stretched a bit too far and the stand taken by the littorals to exclude India from the MSSI is definitely not in consonance with the evolving security requirements in the region. Here, the decision taken by the GCC to actively coordinate their efforts with the extra regional navies in combating piracy in the Gulf of Aden is worthy of emulation. India, as the immediate maritime neighbour and a funnel state, has established a flourishing defence cooperation with the littorals and indicated its willingness to contribute towards augmenting their efforts. It is important that the Indian Navy is involved in the MSSI as a partner to meet the emerging threats and challenges in the region. A security construct under the aegis of IONS, initiated by Australia and India could also be a suitable model for ensuring maritime security in the region.

Endnotes

1. Excerpted from Defence Minister's speech at the fifth International Institute for Strategic Studies Asia Security Summit in Singapore on June 3, 2006.
2. Regional Cooperation on Maritime Piracy: A Prelude to Greater Multilateralism in Asia? *Jennifer C. Bulkeley. Journal of Public and International Affairs*, Volume 14/Spring 2003. Trustees of Princeton University.

3. En.wikipedia.org. Accessed on May 14, 2010.

4. Regional Cooperation On Maritime Piracy:A Prelude To Greater Multilateralism In Asia?*Jennifer C. Bulkeley. Journal of Public and International Affairs*, Volume 14/Spring 2003. Copyright ? 2003, the Trustees of Princeton University. http://www.princeton.edu/~jpia.

5. RSIS Web commentary. Terror in the Malacca Strait: The Risks of Overreaction. Sam Bateman. March 10, 2010.

6. UNCLOS, Montego Bay, December 10, 1982.

7. Maritime Security and the Cooperative Mechanism for the Strait of Malacca and Singapore, Robert Beckman, during the Maritime Conference on 'Between Rising Naval Powers: Implications for SE Asia of the Rise of Chinese and Indian Naval Powers', Singapore, November 18-19, 2008.

8. Ibid. This paragraph is based on the excellent paper presented by Robert Beckman, above.

9. Ibid. Estimate made by Yohei Sasakawa, Chairman of Nippon Foundation, during his speech at the symposium on the enhancement of safety of navigation and the environmental protection of the Strait of Malacca and Singapore', Kuala Lumpur, Malaysia, March 13-14, 2007.

10. Nazery Khalid, "To Serve and to be Protected: A Comprehensive Perspective on Security in the Strait of Malacca", *Maritime Affairs*, Summer Edition, 2009.

11. Ibid.

12. Maritime Security and the Cooperative Mechanism for the Strait of Malacca and Singapore, Robert Beckman, during the Maritime Conference on 'Between Rising Naval Powers: Implications for SE Asia of the Rise of Chinese and Indian Naval Powers', Singapore, November 18-19, 2008.

13. Ibid.

14. Rajiv Sawhney, "Redefining the limits of the Straits- A composite Malacca Strait Security System", IDSS Commentary, May 2006.

CHAPTER – VI

INDIA'S ROLE AND EXPERIENCES IN COMBATING PIRACY

"India's growing international stature gives it strategic relevance in the area ranging from the Persian Gulf to the Strait of Malacca...India has exploited the fluidities of the emerging world order to forge new links through a combination of diplomatic repositioning, economic resurgence and military firmness."

—Dr Manmohan Singh[1]

***

Case Studies of Anti-piracy Operations

India by virtue of its strategic location, astride the 'equatorial pendulum,' and having the largest navy and coast guard service in the Indian Ocean Region, has a key role in combating piracy. Under the Indian Coast Guard Act of 1978, the Indian Coast Guard is mandated to operate within the country's EEZ. Therefore, the Indian Navy is essentially the lead agency dealing with piracy in the IOR. Since end 2008 Indian naval ships have been deployed on anti-piracy missions in the Gulf of Aden where they have given an excellent account of their professionalism. However, in the past both the navy and coast guard have been called upon to participate in anti-piracy operations. Some notable cases studies of anti-piracy operations are enumerated in the succeeding paragraphs.

The MV *Alondra Rainbow* Incident

The incident of MV *Alondra Rainbow* stands out as the first case of the recapture of a hijacked vessel in modern times. The sequence of events in the joint navy and coast guard operation launched for recapture of the vessel are as follows:-

The start point of the incident was the following report by the Piracy Reporting Centre (PRC) of IMB, broadcast on October 27, 1999:

> *"MV Alondra Rainbow departed Kuala Tanjung in Indonesia for Milke in Japan on 22 Oct 99. Vessel suspected to have been pirated"*

A reward of $ 200,000 was announced by the ship owners for recovery of the vessel. The *Alondra Rainbow*, loaded with 7,000 tons of Aluminium ingots had been hijacked by an armed gang of pirates. The 17 crew members (Two Japanese and 15 Filipino) were subsequently transferred to MV *Sanyo* at sea and after being captive for a week, set adrift in a lifeboat on October 29, 1999. The crew was rescued by a Thai fishing boat after 10 days off the coast of the island of Sumatra.

After the initial IMB broadcast, on November 13, 1999, the master of MV *Al Shuhada*, a Saudi Arab flagged merchant vessel reported to the IMB PRC the sighting of a vessel matching the descriptions of MV *Alondra Rainbow*, 66 nautical miles South of Cape Comorin. The information was passed on by the PRC to Indian Coast Guard.

The response of the Indian Coast Guard was swift and Operation 'Nelson' was launched to search and intercept the reported vessel. Under the operation, a Dornier aircraft and a ship were deployed to search and investigate the reported vessel. Other coastguard vessels on patrol at sea were also diverted to the area. The ship was intercepted by the coast guard aircraft and it was observed that the vessel has changed her name to MV *Mega Rama* and was flying the Belize Flag. The pirates initially did not respond to the calls on radio. However, subsequently they responded stating, that the vessel MV *Mega Rama* was bound from Manila to Al Fujairah, UAE. All the other details furnished by the ship were also fictitious. These were verified by the IMB.

The ship was kept under surveillance till a Coast Guard ship arrived on the scene. However, despite warning shots fired across the bows, the ship increased speed and continued on its course. Subsequently, a naval ship INS Prahar (missile corvette) was deployed to assist the coast guard in interdicting the ship through the use of superior naval firepower. The ship was successfully apprehended and the 15 Indonesian hijackers onboard arrested by the coast guard. The pirates had attempted to scuttle the ship by flooding the engine room and also set it on fire. Later when IN Ships *Gomati* and *Delhi* arrived on the scene, the naval boarding party extinguished the fire onboard, brought the flooding under control and prepared the ship to be taken under tow assisted by CG Ships. The *Alondra Rainbow* was eventually towed by a Coast Guard ship to Mumbai, arriving there on November 21, 1999[2].

Investigations revealed that on October 23, 1999 the master and 14 crew had changed the name of the vessel to *Global Venture* and proceeded to Miri in East Malaysia, arriving there on October 26. Her hull was repainted from the original blue to black. On October 27 about 3,000 tons of Aluminum ingots were transshipped to another ship called *Bonsoon II*, which came alongside. Subsequently, the ship was directed by the employment agent to towards Karachi, Pakistan. At some stage, the name of the vessel was changed to *Mega Rama*[3].

The incident of the *Alondra Rainbow* highlighted the importance of timely alerts by IMB, the vigilance of the crew members who first sighted the vessel and the prompt reporting by the masters. Without the swift response of the Indian Coast Guard and the seamless coordination with navy, perhaps, the operation may not have been successful.

Operation Sagittarius

Soon after the terrorist attacks on the World Trade Centre and the Pentagon in the United States, Washington requested New Delhi in October 2001 to support the international war on terrorism by undertaking escort duties in the Malacca Strait. Piracy in the Malacca Strait had peaked at his point of time and there was a clear and present danger of pirates and terrorists attacking high value USN targets. Consequently, under Operation Sagittarius, Indian naval ships engaged in escorting US flagged high value vessels through the Strait. Indian Naval Ships escorted 24 US vessels between April 2 and September 16, 2002[4]. The high value units included a nuclear submarine and some US naval auxiliaries. The area of operation included the Andaman Sea, Malacca Straits and the South China Sea. This was the first time that an Indian naval ship was carrying out such escort operations since the 1971 Indo-Pakistan War.[5]

Hijacking of the Indian Dhow *Bhakti Sagar*

An Indian Dhow *Bhakti Sagar* registered in Porbandar, India was captured by armed pirates off Somalia on February 26, 2006 and its crew of 25 Indian sailors held hostage pending demand for a huge ransom. The dhow was crusing along the East coast of Africa to Kismayu, when it was hijacked by armed Somali pirates. By February 28 the dhow had been anchored off Harradere, Somalia. The crew were held hostage onboard by with eight armed pirates.

INS *Mumbai* which was returning from a goodwill visit to Salalah, Oman was diverted by the navy for assistance. The ship could reach the area only by March 13, 2006. Fortunately coinciding with the arrival of the ship, ongoing third party negotiations yielded results and on March 16 the crew members were released[6].

Anti-piracy Patrols in the Gulf of Aden

Following the incident of MV *Stolt Valor*[7] the Government of India decided to deploy Indian Naval ships on anti-piracy patrols in the Gulf of Aden region. On November 10, 2008 INS *Tabar* whilst on an anti-piracy patrol in the Gulf of Aden successfully prevented a piracy attack on MV *Jag Arnav* of Great Eastern Shipping Company. The sequence of events in the operation were as follows:-

- MV *Jag Arnav*, a 38,265-tonne dry bulk carrier whilst about 60 nautical miles off East of Aden, spotted (around 1030 hours local time) pirates armed with automatic weapons approaching the vessel on speed boats. The vessel raised an alarm.
- INS *Tabar* which was on patrol about 25 nautical miles away from the merchant vessel immediately

launched an armed helicopter with marine commandos to intervene and prevent the pirates from boarding and hijacking the merchant vessel.

- The attempt by the pirates to hijack the vessel was successfully foiled by marine commandos of INS *Tabar*. Thereafter, INS *Tabar* moved closer to the vessel to escort her safely. Subsequently, it came to light that the actions of INS *Tabar* also averted a possible attack - by the same pirates - on the Saudi flagged MV *Thihama* which was located close to MV *Jag Arnab*.

On November 18, 2008, about 285 nautical miles South West of Salalah (Oman), INS *Tabar* noticed a suspicious vessel similar to mother ships used by Somali pirates with two speed boats in tow. When INS *Tabar* closed in and asked the vessel to stop for investigation, the pirates with guns and Rocket Propelled Grenade launchers threatened to blow up INS *Tabar* and commenced indiscriminate firing on the warship.

INS *Tabar* returned fire in self-defence and a major fire broke out on the pirate vessel. A series of explosions were heard, possibly due to exploding ammunition that was stored on the pirate vessel and subsequently the pirate ship sank.

Latest Developments

The Indian Navy crossed a milestone in out-of-area operations in June 2010 when it safely escorted its thousandth ship; the MV *Bornza*, through the Gulf of Aden. The Indian navy has been deployed in the International Maritime Transit Corridor off the Horn of Africa and the coast of Somalia since October 2008, making it the navy's longest continuous out-of-area deployment ever.

More than 24 ships (as in January 2011) have been deployed in the region on anti-piracy patrols[8].

As on January 25, 2011 the Indian naval ships had safely escorted a total of 1,487 ships, including 1,321 foreign flagged vessels from different countries. 26 piracy attempts have been thwarted and no ship under Indian escort has been hijacked by pirates. The anti-piracy patrols are in addition to the regular Exclusive Economic Zone patrols conducted by the Indian navy in the waters off the Maldives and the Seychelles[9].

Anti-piracy Operations off Lakshadweep: On January 30, 2011 the Indian Navy and the Coast Guard in a joint operation intercepted and neutralised *Prantalay* a Thai fishing vessel, which was being used by Somali pirates as 'mother vessel' since April 2010 for piracy at various locations in the Arabian Sea.[10] The sequence of events is narrated below:

- A Coast Guard Dornier while responding to a Mayday call from MV *Verdi*, a Bahama Flagged container ship, located two skiffs attempting a piracy attack. Seeing the aircraft, the skiffs immediately aborted their piracy attempt and dashed towards the mother vessel *Prantalay* which hurriedly hoisted the two skiffs onboard and set a Westerly course to escape from the area.

- While Coast Guard and Naval Dorniers continuously tracked *Prantalay*, an Indian Naval Ship already deployed in the area for anti-piracy patrol - was directed to intercept and investigate.

- The naval ship closed on to *Prantalay* and made all efforts to establish communication on the international Mercantile Marine Band, but the vessel did not respond and continued to proceed Westwards.

- In keeping with internationally accepted norms, the warship fired a warning shot well ahead of the bows of *Prantalay* to compel her to stop. Instead of stopping, however, *Prantalay* suddenly opened fire on the warship. The naval ship returned limited fire in self-defence. A fire broke out on *Prantalay* (mother vessels are known to carry additional fuel drums to fuel the skiffs) and the 'personnel were seen jumping overboard.
- Twenty Thai and Myanmarese fishermen, the original crew of the vessel, who had been held hostage by the pirates for over eight months and 15 pirates, were pulled out from the waters by the naval ship. The arrested pirates were handed over to the Police Mumbai for investigations.

In recent months the Somali pirates – in an attempt to avoid the multinational naval forces in the Gulf of Aden - have extended their area of operations to upto 1350 miles from the Somali coast and have carried out several attacks on ships close to India. This poses a serious challenge for India and calls for continuous surveillance efforts in the region by both the navy and Coast Guard.

Indian Ocean Naval Symposium (IONS)

With a view to achieving assured and mutually beneficial maritime security, stability, safety and consequent collective prosperity amongst all littoral states of the IOR, the 21st century's first regional maritime security initiative, was launched on February 15, 2008. The IONS was the result of bold initiatives taken by the Indian Navy and the National Maritime Foundation and is based on the recognition of the centrality of 'Constructive Engagement' involving all regional states. The IONS provides a regional forum through which the Chiefs of the regional navies (and/or the principal maritime agencies responsible for maritime security) of all the littoral states of the IOR can periodically meet to constructively engage one another. The inaugural session of the IONS was attended by 27 Chiefs-of-Navy from the 35 member states of the IOR.

Aim

The primary aim of 'IONS' is to sustain a regionally relevant, consultative forum within which the navies (and/or the principal maritime agencies responsible for maritime security) of the littoral States of the IOR, along with such other relevant maritime entities as may be agreed upon from time-to-time by the members, can discuss issues and concerns that bear upon maritime security, with a view to arriving at agreed courses of action on trans-national issues, based upon a common understanding of the regional maritime security environment.

Objectives

The key objectives of the IONS are as follows:

- To promote a shared understanding of issues and concerns relevant to the IOR which bear upon maritime security.
- To strengthen the capability of all nation-states of the IOR to address present and anticipated challenges to maritime security and stability.
- To establish and promote a variety of trans-national, maritime, consultative and cooperative mechanisms, designed to address and mitigate maritime security-concerns of the IOR.
- To develop interoperability in terms of doctrines, strategies, procedures, organisational and logistic systems, and, operational processes, so as to promote

the provision of speedy, responsive, and effective Humanitarian Assistance and Disaster-Relief (HADR) throughout the IOR.

The second session of the IONs was held in May 2010 at Abu Dhabi, UAE, under the theme 'Together, for the Reinforcement of Maritime Security in the Indian Ocean.' The IONS-2 was attended by representatives from 27 navies of the IOR and the Chairmanship of the IONS passed over from the Indian navy to the UAE navy. In its two years of existence, the IONS has been hugely supported by the Indian Navy and various activities aimed at promoting close navy to navy ties, as envisaged in its original charter were conducted by member states. Some notable events are as below:

- Open Essay Competition conducted by the Indian Navy in 2008.
- IONS Technical Seminar – 2009 conducted by the Sri Lankan navy at Colombo.

IONS -2 preparatory workshop conducted by the Kenyan navy in October 2009.

Thus, in its short period of existence of two years, the IONS has emerged as a viable regional forum for addressing the challenges of piracy in the IOR. While, much remains to be achieved on ground, it is opined that in the near future, the IONS could potentially evolve a regional framework or construct for combating piracy in the IOR.

Endnotes

1. Freedom to use the seas: India's Maritime Military Strategy, IHQ MoD (Navy), 2007.
2. Interaction with Coast Guard officers at the ICG HQs.

3. OP Sharma. The International Law of the Sea, India and the UN Convention of 1982. OUP 2009, New Delhi.

4. Vijay Sakhuja. Naval Diplomacy; Indian Initiatives. www.bharat-rakshak.com. Accessed on June 14, 2010.

5. www.mod.nic.in/samachar. Accessed on June 10, 2010.

6. Admiral (Retd) Arun Prakash. The Menace of Piracy, India, the International Community and an UN Response. www.acus.org. Accessed on June 23, 2010.

7. The MT *Stolt Valor* was a Japanese owned Chemical Tanker under Hong Kong Flag that was hijacked on September 15, 2008 by Somali pirates while in the Designated Safety Corridor within the Gulf of Aden approximately 38 nautical miles away from the coast of Yemen., while heading from the United States through the Gulf towards Asia.

8. Statement by Ambassador HS Ppuri, Permanent representative of India on 'Piracy off the coast of Somalia' at the UN Security Council on January 25, 2011. Http://www.un.int/india/2011/ind1815.pdf. Accessed on February 01, 2011.

9. The Telegraph. Kolkata. June 20, 2010.

10. http://www.ndtv.com/article/india/indian-navy-coast-guard-rescue-thai-vessel-from-pirates-82219. Accessed on January 31, 2011.

Chapter – VII

Policy Options for India

"...As military forces of India, we would be expected to function as instruments of peace and stability in this rather fragile environment of the Indian Ocean Region. We have to get our 'hands dirty' in addressing common concerns in our respective domains. This will call for increased participation in peace operations, efforts such as anti-piracy as also capacity-building and capability-enhancement of smaller and economically weaker nations which look up to us, for support and security."

—Admiral (Retired) Sureesh Mehta[1]

The challenges posed by piracy in the IOR to India are multi-faceted and complex. India is geographically located between the Gulf of Aden and the Strait of Malacca regions, astride the main shipping route or 'equatorial pendulum'. Nearly, 90% of India's trade by volume and 77 % by value is seaborne. 40% of the seaborne trade transits through the Strait of Malacca and about 50 % through the Gulf of Aden region[2]; both trouble spots in the IOR. Further, India has the seventeenth largest merchant fleet in the world and provides over 6% of the manpower (approximately 100,000 seafarers) to the global shipping industry[3]. Therefore, the primary challenges for India are to ensure security of its shipping fleet, seaborne trade and safety of Indian seafarers. As the largest country in the region; in terms of population, size (except for Australia), GDP and naval power India is also expected to play a key role in combating piracy in the IOR. Thus, India is presented with a unique opportunity to further its foreign interests in the region by playing a key role in combating piracy in the IOR. This role was played by the British and Dutch naval forces in the 19th century, when piracy was prevalent in Southeast Asia.

India currently does not have a stated anti-piracy policy that seeks to protect India's seaborne trade and that which addresses the concerns of seafarers from India and other countries of the region. The decision of the Indian government to deploy a warship in the Gulf of Aden in early 2009 was in response to the protests from the families of the Indian crew onboard the MV *Stolt Valor*, which was hijacked on September 15, 2008 by Somali pirates. The *Stolt Valor* was a Japanese owned vessel, managed by a Hongkong based company, carrying cargo for a US customer. Its only Indian connection being that 18 of the 21 crew (including Master) were Indians. The ship was subsequently released of payment of ransom money. During the negotiations, it was the Indian government which was at the forefront of the negotiations with the pirates with the Flag State representatives in the background. This was contrary to the spirit of UNCLOS, Article 94 (see Annexure 1) that mandates the Flag State to take responsibility for safety and security of its ship and crew. The Indian Naval warships deployed in the Gulf of Aden region have since, safely escorted over a thousand ships and successfully thwarted several piracy attempts, even destroying some 'mother' ships used by Somali pirates. However, the deployment of a single warship has in no way reduced the attacks on Indian seafarers. It was reported that out of the 178[4] crew held hostage by Somali pirates as on March 31, 2010, 95[5] were Indians. Three months later, as on July 07, 2010 six vessels (including Indian Dhows and Foreign ships) with 57 Indian crew were held hostage by the Somali pirates[6]. According to IMB, in 2010, 1181 sailors, were taken hostage by pirates worldwide, of which the Somali attacks accounted for 1,016 hostages.

Currently, the shipping industry is largely dominated by the European countries in terms of vessel ownership. The work force is largely from Asian developing countries. The nationalities of the crew currently held hostage by Somalia pirates provides an insight into this aspect. It includes; Bulgaria, Myanmar, Philippines, Ghana, Greece, India, South Korea, Pakistan, Sudan, Sri Lanka, Turkey and Ukraine[7] (as reported in April 2010). The evolution of the shipping industry into fewer and larger cooperative multinational enterprises has led to increasing propensity on part of ship-owners to shoulder the burden of safety and security of the ship and crew. Currently, these risks are transferred to the insurance companies. As seen in the Gulf of Aden, the system of ransom money being paid by the insurance companies has evolved into a lucrative business model for both the pirates and the insurance companies, with the costs being passed on to the end consumers.

Clearly, such a trend is dangerous in the long term since it does not address the interests of the crew. It is opined, that this trend will lead to increasing pressure on the navies to provide security. Thus, as the shipping industry evolves into multinational corporations, so will the navies have to evolve cooperative security mechanisms to address the security concerns (Perhaps, signs of this evolution process can be seen in the Gulf of Aden where more than 20 warships in - four different alliances - from over 14 navies are currently operating on anti-piracy patrols).

Policy Options

It is evident that the maritime environment in the IOR is unlikely to change in the near to mid term nor will it be entirely possible to eradicate piracy from the IOR. Therefore, the best policy options would be that which help minimise the number of attacks on Indian seafarers and ships to a low and acceptable level such that, it continues to inspire Indian citizens to seek a carrier in the maritime industry. There are five main policy options for India to consider.

- First, India should leverage its close ties and naval cooperation with Southeast Asian littorals and Australia to establish a regional security construct in the region. This could be achieved under the aegis of the IONS and seek to augment the surveillance efforts of the littoral navies; currently overwhelmed with the task of securing the straits under the Malacca Strait Patrols. Presently, regional sensitivities of Indonesia and Malaysia preclude extra regional participation in the ongoing security mechanism. A security mechanism involving Australia - also a major stakeholder in the safety and security of the straits - could help to allay the fears of extra regional domination in the minds of the littorals and also offset some of the costs.

- Secondly, in the Gulf of Aden, Indian should work with like-minded Gulf States to evolve a regional cooperative mechanism under the IONS. India should actively assist the African states involved in the Djibouti Code of Conduct which seeks to establish a mechanism for information sharing, training and capacity building. India should also enhance the anti-piracy patrols in the Gulf of Aden region and offer to provide assistance for Bangladeshi and Sri Lankan seafarers.
- Thirdly, India should raise the issue of piracy in the Gulf of Aden in the UN General Assembly and highlight the inadequacy of extant legal framework in ensuring the trial and detention of Somali pirates. While, Russia has already introduced this issue in the UN Security Council and the Contact Group on Piracy off the Coast off Somalia (chaired by Denmark) - established under UN Resolution 1851/ 2009 - and the EU are also concurrently examining this issue, it is opined that a debate on the issue of prosecution of Somali pirates in the UN General Assembly would perhaps lead to a wider consensus. In the words of C. Raja Mohan, India's leading strategic thinker[8]; "for long India has been a rule taker and as the emerging third largest economy of the world the time has come for India to play the role of a rule maker."
- Fourthly, India should also seek to develop affordable onboard ship security devices such as the electrified fencing systems, Long Range Acoustic Device, etc. This could be done on a public private partnership basis. Further, under the aegis of IONS, India could also consider conducting workshops on best practices for onboard security and international exhibitions for ship security systems. A training centre for ship security could be also be established in India for the benefit of all regional

states.

- Finally, India should press for the shipping industry to invest in onboard private security regulated by the IMO and also encourage Indian flagged ships to invest in private security. The high seas aren't any safer than lonely stretches of highways on land where highway robbers prowl. A certain minimum deterrence could go a long way in reducing the number of successful piracy attacks. However, at the international level, private security onboard ships would require formulation of a new set of uniform regulations regarding carriage of firearms onboard, rules of engagement for private security teams, etc. Perhaps, a system for ensuring a certain minimum 'hardening' of ships could be considered on lines of the ISPS code of 2004, which mandated ships and ports to adopt certain security guidelines promulgated by the IMO. It may be recalled, that the implementation of the ISPS code was initially met with huge resistance from the shipping industry; however, the IMO went ahead with the programme. In its five years the ISPS code has proved to be an invaluable tool for the shipping industry. Perhaps, a similar approach would have to be adopted by IMO to implement regulations for 'hardening' of ships.

The above policy options for India seek to reduce the impact of piracy on India's seaborne trade and protect Indian seafarers. They also provide an opportunity to promote India's strategic interests in the IOR. However, in the end, it is opined; whatever be the choice of policy option(s) that the Indian government exercises, it is imperative that the same is well articulated and emphasised. A well articulated policy will invite greater participation from the various stakeholders including the Indian shipping sector and the industry and help offset costs. More importantly, it will clarify the misperceptions that might be extant in parts of India's maritime neighbourhood in combating the non-traditional threats in the IOR.

Endnotes

1. Address by Admiral Sureesh Mehta at the India Habitat Centre, New Delhi on August 10, 2009. 'India's National Security Challenges – An Armed Forces Overview.'
2. www.telegraphindia.com. Accessed on June 19, 2010.
3. Ministry of Shipping, Annual Report 2009.
4. ICC IMB Piracy and Armed Robbery Against Ships, Report for the Period January 1 to March 31, 2010, p 18.
5. www.bartamana.com. Source AFP. Accessed on April 11, 2010.
6. Based on Maritime Rescue Coordination Centre, Mumbai, reports and interaction with CG officers.
7. Interaction with Cyrus Mody, Manager IMB, London.
8. C Raja Mohan, Strategic Affairs Editor, *The Indian Express*, New Delhi. During a lecture at the National Maritime Foundation, New Delhi on July 19, 2010 titled 'India and the Changing Geopolitics of the Indian Ocean.'

ANNEXURE – I

UNITED NATIONS CONVENTION ON THE LAW OF THE SEA OF DECEMBER 10, 1982: EXCERPTS OF ARTICLES RELEVANT TO PIRACY

Article 94

Duties of the flag State

1. Every State shall effectively exercise its jurisdiction and control in administrative, technical and social matters over ships flying its flag.
2. In particular every State shall:
   (a) maintain a register of ships containing the names and particulars of ships flying its flag, except those which are excluded from generally accepted international regulations on account of their small size; and

(b) assume jurisdiction under its internal law over each ship flying its flag and its master, officers and crew in respect of administrative, technical and social matters concerning the ship.

3. Every State shall take such measures for ships flying its flag as are necessary to ensure safety at sea with regard, *inter alia*, to:

(a) the construction, equipment and seaworthiness of ships;

(b) the manning of ships, labour conditions and the training of crews, taking into account the applicable international instruments;

(c) the use of signals, the maintenance of communications and the prevention of collisions.

4. Such measures shall include those necessary to ensure:

(a) that each ship, before registration and thereafter at appropriate intervals, is surveyed by a qualified surveyor of ships, and has on board such charts, nautical publications and navigational equipment and instruments as are appropriate for the safe navigation of the ship;

(b) that each ship is in the charge of a master and officers who possess appropriate qualifications, in particular in seamanship, navigation, communications and marine engineering, and that the crew is appropriate in qualification and numbers for the type, size, machinery and equipment of the ship;

(c) that the master, officers and, to the extent appropriate, the crew are fully conversant with and required to observe the applicable international regulations concerning the safety of life at sea, the prevention of collisions, the prevention, reduction and control of marine pollution, and the maintenance of communications by radio.

5. In taking the measures called for in paragraphs 3 and 4 each State is required to conform to generally accepted international regulations, procedures and practices and to take any steps which may be necessary to secure their observance.
6. A State which has clear grounds to believe that proper jurisdiction and control with respect to a ship have not been exercised may report the facts to the flag State. Upon receiving such a report, the flag State shall investigate the matter and, if appropriate, take any action necessary to remedy the situation.
7. Each State shall cause an inquiry to be held by or before a suitably qualified person or persons into every marine casualty or incident of navigation on the high seas involving a ship flying its flag and causing loss of life or serious injury to nationals of another State or serious damage to ships or installations of another State or to the marine environment. The flag State and the other State shall cooperate in the conduct of any inquiry held by that other State into any such marine casualty or incident of navigation.

***

Article100

Duty to cooperate in the repression of piracy

All States shall cooperate to the fullest possible extent in the repression of piracy on the high seas or in any other place outside the jurisdiction of any State.

***

Article101

Definition of piracy

Piracy consists of any of the following acts:

(a) any illegal acts of violence or detention, or any act

of depredation, committed for private ends by the crew or the passengers of a private ship or a private aircraft, and directed:

(i) on the high seas, against another ship or aircraft, or against persons or property on board such ship or aircraft;

(ii) against a ship, aircraft, persons or property in a place outside the jurisdiction of any State;

(b) any act of voluntary participation in the operation of a ship or of an aircraft with knowledge of facts making it a pirate ship or aircraft;

(c) any act of inciting or of intentionally facilitating an act described in subparagraph (a) or (b).

***

Article 102

Piracy by a warship, government ship or government aircraft whose crew has mutinied

The acts of piracy, as defined in article 101, committed by a warship, government ship or government aircraft whose crew has mutinied and taken control of the ship or aircraft are assimilated to acts committed by a private ship or aircraft.

***

Article 103

Definition of a pirate ship or aircraft

A ship or aircraft is considered a pirate ship or aircraft if it is intended by the persons in dominant control to be used for the purpose of committing one of the acts referred to in article 101. The same applies if the ship or aircraft has been used to commit any such act, so long as it remains under the control of the persons guilty of that act.

***

Article 104

Retention or loss of the nationality of a pirate ship or aircraft

A ship or aircraft may retain its nationality although it has become a pirate ship or aircraft. The retention or loss of nationality is determined by the law of the State from which such nationality was derived.

***

Article 105

Seizure of a pirate ship or aircraft

On the high seas, or in any other place outside the jurisdiction of any State, every State may seize a pirate ship or aircraft, or a ship or aircraft taken by piracy and under the control of pirates, and arrest the persons and seize the property on board. The courts of the State which carried out the seizure may decide upon the penalties to be imposed, and may also determine the action to be taken with regard to the ships, aircraft or property, subject to the rights of third parties acting in good faith.

***

Article 106

Liability for seizure without adequate grounds

Where the seizure of a ship or aircraft on suspicion of piracy has been effected without adequate grounds, the State making the seizure shall be liable to the State the nationality of which is possessed by the ship or aircraft for any loss or damage caused by the seizure.

***

Article 107

Ships and aircraft which are entitled to seize on account of piracy

A seizure on account of piracy may be carried out only by warships or military aircraft, or other ships or aircraft clearly marked and identifiable as being on government service and authorized to that effect.

***

Article 110

Right of visit

1. Except where acts of interference derive from powers conferred by treaty, a warship which encounters on the high seas a foreign ship, other than a ship entitled to complete immunity in accordance with articles 95 and 96, is not justified in boarding it unless there is reasonable ground for suspecting that:

   (a) the ship is engaged in piracy;

   (b) the ship is engaged in the slave trade;

   (c) the ship is engaged in unauthorized broadcasting and the flag State of the warship has jurisdiction under article 109;

   (d) the ship is without nationality; or

   (e) though flying a foreign flag or refusing to show its flag, the ship is, in reality, of the same nationality as the warship.

2. In the cases provided for in paragraph 1, the warship may proceed to verify the ship's right to fly its flag. To this end, it may send a boat under the command of an officer to the suspected ship. If suspicion remains after the documents have been checked, it may proceed to a further examination on board the ship, which must be carried out with all possible consideration.

3. If the suspicions prove to be unfounded, and provided that the ship boarded has not committed any act justifying them, it shall be compensated for any loss or damage that may have been sustained.

4. These provisions apply *mutatis mutandis* to military aircraft.

5. These provisions also apply to any other duly authorized ships or aircraft clearly marked and identifiable as being on government service.

ANNEXURE – II

CONVENTION FOR THE SUPPRESSION OF UNLAWFUL ACTS AGAINST THE SAFETY OF MARITIME NAVIGATION

(ROME, 10 MARCH 1988)

THE STATES PARTIES TO THIS CONVENTION,

HAVING IN MIND: the purposes and principles of the Charter of the United Nations concerning the maintenance of international peace and security and the promotion of friendly relations and co-operation among States,

RECOGNIZING: in particular that everyone has the right to life, liberty and security of person, as set out in the Universal Declaration of Human Rights and the International Covenant on Civil and Political Rights,

DEEPLY CONCERNED: about the world-wide escalation of acts of terrorism in all its forms, which endanger or take innocent human lives, jeopardize fundamental freedoms and seriously impair the dignity of human beings,

CONSIDERING: that unlawful acts against the safety of maritime navigation jeopardize the safety of persons and property, seriously affect the operation of maritime services, and undermine the confidence of the peoples of the world in the safety of maritime navigation,

CONSIDERING: that the occurrence of such acts is a matter of grave concern to the international community as a whole,

BEING CONVINCED: of the urgent need to develop international co-operation between States in devising and adopting effective and practical measures for the prevention of all unlawful acts against the safety of maritime navigation, and the prosecution and punishment of their perpetrators,

RECALLING: resolution 40/61 of the General Assembly of the United Nations of 9 December 1985 which, *inter alia*, "urges all States unilaterally and in co-operation with other States, as well as relevant United Nations organs, to contribute to the progressive elimination of causes underlying international terrorism and to pay special attention to all situations, including colonialism, racism and situations involving mass and flagrant violations of human rights and fundamental freedoms and those involving alien occupation, that may give rise to international terrorism and may endanger international peace and security",

RECALLING FURTHER: that resolution 40/61 "unequivocally condemns, as criminal, all acts, methods and practices of terrorism wherever and by whomever committed, including those which jeopardize friendly relations among States and their security",

RECALLING ALSO: that by resolution 40/61, the International Maritime Organization was invited to "study the problem of terrorism aboard or against ships with a view to making recommendations on appropriate measures",

HAVING IN MIND: resolution A.584(14) of 20 November 1985, of the Assembly of the International Maritime Organization, which called for development of measures to prevent unlawful acts which threaten the safety of ships and the security of their passengers and crews,

NOTING: that acts of the crew which are subject to normal shipboard discipline are outside the purview of this Convention,

AFFIRMING: the desirability of monitoring rules and standards relating to the prevention and control of unlawful acts against ships and persons on board ships, with a view to updating them as necessary, and, to this effect, taking note with satisfaction of the Measures to Prevent Unlawful Acts against Passengers and Crews on Board Ships, recommended by the Maritime Safety Committee of the International Maritime Organization,

AFFIRMING FURTHER: that matters not regulated by this Convention continue to be governed by the rules and principles of general international law,

RECOGNIZING: the need for all States, in combating unlawful acts against the safety of maritime navigation, strictly to comply with rules and principles of general international law,

HAVE AGREED: *as follows:*

Article 1

For the purposes of this Convention, "ship" means a vessel of any type whatsoever not permanently attached to the sea-bed, including dynamically supported craft, submersibles, or any other floating craft.

Article 2

1. This Convention does not apply to:
   (a) a warship; or
   (b) a ship owned or operated by a State when being used as a naval auxiliary or for customs or police purposes; or
   (c) a ship which has been withdrawn from navigation or laid up.
2. Nothing in this Convention affects the immunities of warships and other government ships operated for non-commercial purposes.

Article 3

1. Any person commits an offence if that person unlawfully and intentionally:
   (a) seizes or exercises control over a ship by force or threat thereof or any other form of intimidation; or
   (b) performs an act of violence against a person on board a ship if that act is likely to endanger the safe navigation of that ship; or
   (c) destroys a ship or causes damage to a ship or to its cargo which is likely to endanger the safe navigation of that ship; or
   (d) places or causes to be placed on a ship, by any means whatsoever, a device or substance which

is likely to destroy that ship, or cause damage to that ship or its cargo which endangers or is likely to endanger the safe navigation of that ship; or

(e) destroys or seriously damages maritime navigational facilities or seriously interferes with their operation, if any such act is likely to endanger the safe navigation of a ship; or

(f) communicates information which he knows to be false, thereby endangering the safe navigation of a ship; or

(g) injures or kills any person, in connection with the commission or the attempted commission of any of the offences set forth in subparagraphs (a) to (f).

2. Any person also commits an offence if that person:

(a) attempts to commit any of the offences set forth in paragraph 1; or

(b) abets the commission of any of the offences set forth in paragraph 1 perpetrated by any person or is otherwise an accomplice of a person who commits such an offence; or

(c) threatens, with or without a condition, as is provided for under national law, aimed at compelling a physical or juridical person to do or refrain from doing any act, to commit any of the offences set forth in paragraph 1, subparagraphs (b), (c) and (e), if that threat is likely to endanger the safe navigation of the ship in question.

Article 4

1. This Convention applies if the ship is navigating or is scheduled to navigate into, through or from waters beyond the outer limit of the territorial sea of a single State, or the lateral limits of its territorial sea with adjacent States.

2. In cases where the Convention does not apply pursuant to paragraph 1, it nevertheless applies when the offender or the alleged offender is found in the territory of a State Party other than the State referred to in paragraph 1.

Article 5

Each State Party shall mkae the offences set forth in article 3 punishable by appropriate penalties which take into account the grave nature of those offences.

Article 6

1. Each State Party shall take such measures as may be necessary to establish its jurisdiction over the offences set forth in article 3 when the offence is committed:

   (a) against or on board a ship flying the flag of the State at the time the offence is committed; or

   (b) in the territory of that State, including its territorial sea; or

   (c) by a national of that State.

2. A State Party may also establish its jurisdiction over any such offence when:

   (a) it is committed by a stateless person whose habitual residence is in that State; or

   (b) during its commission a national of that State is seized, threatened, injured or killed; or

   (c) it is committed in an attempt to compel that State to do or abstain from doing any act.

3. Any State Party which has established jurisdiction mentioned in paragraph 2 shall notify the Secretary-General of the International Maritime Organization (hereinafter referred to as "the Secretary-General").

If such State Party subsequently rescinds that jurisdiction, it shall notify the Secretary-General.

4. Each State Party shall take such measures as may be necessary to establish its jurisdiction over the offences set forth in article 3 in cases where the alleged offender is present in its territory and it does not extradite him to any of the States Parties which have established their jurisdiction in accordance with paragraphs 1 and 2 of this article.

5. This Convention does not exclude any criminal jurisdiction exercised in accordance with national law.

Article 7

1. Upon being satisfied that the circumstances so warrant, any State Party in the territory of which the offender or the alleged offender is present shall, in accordance with its law, take him into custody or take other measures to ensure his presence for such time as is necessary to enable any criminal or extradition proceedings to be instituted.

2. Such State shall immediately make a preliminary inquiry into the facts, in accordance with its own legislation.

3. Any person regarding whom the measures referred to in paragraph 1 are being taken shall be entitled to:

   (a) communicate without delay with the nearest appropriate representative of the State of which he is a national or which is otherwise entitled to establish such communication or, if he is a stateless person, the State in the territory of which he has his habitual residence;

   (b) be visited by a representative of that State.

4. The rights referred to in paragraph 3 shall be exercised in conformity with the laws and

regulations of the State in the territory of which the offender or the alleged offender is present, subject to the proviso that the said laws and regulations must enable full effect to be given to the purposes for which the rights accorded under paragraph 3 are intended.

5. When a State Party, pursuant to this article, has taken a person into custody, it shall immediately notify the States which have established jurisdiction in accordance with article 6, paragraph 1 and, if it considers it advisable, any other interested States, of the fact that such person is in custody and of the circumstances which warrant his detention. The State which makes the preliminary inquiry contemplated in paragraph 2 of this article shall promptly report its findings to the said States and shall indicate whether it intends to exercise jurisdiction.

Article 8

1. The master of a ship of a State Party (the "flag State") may deliver to the authorities of any other State Party (the "receiving State") any person who he has reasonable grounds to believe has committed one of the offences set forth in article 3.

2. The flag State shall ensure that the master of its ship is obliged, whenever practicable, and if possible before entering the territorial sea of the receiving State carrying on board any person whom the master intends to deliver in accordance with paragraph 1, to give notification to the authorities of the receiving State of his intention to deliver such person and the reasons therefor.

3. The receiving State shall accept the delivery, except where it has grounds to consider that the Convention is not applicable to the acts giving rise to the delivery, and shall proceed in accordance

with the provisions of article 7. Any refusal to accept a delivery shall be accompanied by a statement of the reasons for refusal.

4. The flag State shall ensure that the master of its ship is obliged to furnish the authorities of the receiving State with the evidence in the master's possession which pertains to the alleged offence.

5. A receiving State which has accepted the delivery of a person in accordance with paragraph 3 may, in turn, request the flag State to accept delivery of that person. The flag State shall consider any such request, and if it accedes to the request it shall proceed in accordance with article 7. If the flag State declines a request, it shall furnish the receiving State with a statement of the reasons there for.

Article 9

Nothing in this Convention shall affect in any way the rules of international law pertaining to the competence of States to exercise investigative or enforcement jurisdiction on board ships not flying their flag.

Article 10

1. The State Party in the territory of which the offender or the alleged offender is found shall, in cases to which article 6 applies, if it does not extradite him, be obliged, without exception whatsoever and whether or not the offence was committed in its territory, to submit the case without delay to its competent authorities for the purpose of prosecution, through proceedings in accordance with the laws of that State. Those authorities shall take their decision in the same manner as in the case of any other offence of a grave nature under the law of that State.

2. Any person regarding whom proceedings are being carried out in connection with any of the offences

set forth in article 3 shall be guaranteed fair treatment at all stages of the proceedings, including enjoyment of all the rights and guarantees provided for such proceedings by the law of the State in the territory of which he is present.

Article 11

1. The offences set forth in article 3 shall be deemed to be included as extraditable offences in any extradition treaty existing between any of the States Parties. States Parties undertake to include such offences as extraditable offences in every extradition treaty to be concluded between them.
2. If a State Party which makes extradition conditional on the existence of a treaty receives a request for extradition from another State Party with which it has no extradition treaty, the requested State Party may, at its option, consider this Convention as a legal basis for extradition in respect of the offences set forth in article 3. Extradition shall be subject to the other conditions provided by the law of the requested State Party.
3. States Parties which do not make extradition conditional on the existence of a treaty shall recognize the offences set forth in article 3 as extraditable offences between themselves, subject to the conditions provided by the law of the requested State.
4. If necessary, the offences set forth in article 3 shall be treated, for the purposes of extradition between States Parties, as if they had been committed not only in the place in which they occurred but also in a place within the jurisdiction of the State Party requesting extradition.
5. A State Party which receives more than one request for extradition from States which have established jurisdiction in accordance with article 6[1]and which decides not to prosecute shall, in selecting

the State to which the offender or alleged offender is to be extradited, pay due regard to the interests and responsibilities of the State Party whose flag the ship was flying at the time of the commission of the offence.

6. In considering a request for the extradition of an alleged offender pursuant to this Convention, the requested State shall pay due regard to whether his rights as set forth in article 7, paragraph 3, can be effected in the requesting State.

7. With respect to the offences as defined in this Convention, the provisions of all extradition treaties and arrangements applicable between States Parties are modified as between States Parties to the extent that they are incompatible with this Convention.

Article 12

1. State Parties shall afford one another the greatest measure of assistance in connection with criminal proceedings brought in respect of the offences set forth in article 3, including assistance in obtaining evidence at their disposal necessary for the proceedings.

2. States Parties shall carry out their obligations under paragraph 1 in conformity with any treaties on mutual assistance that may exist between them. In the absence of such treaties, States Parties shall afford each other assistance in accordance with their national law.

Article 13

1. States Parties shall co-operate in the prevention of the offences set forth in article 3, particularly by:

(a) taking all practicable measures to prevent preparations in their respective territories for the commission of those offences within or outside their territories;

(b) exchanging information in accordance with their national law, and co-ordinating administrative and other measures taken as appropriate to prevent the commission of offences set forth in article 3.

2. When, due to the commission of an offence set forth in article 3, the passage of a ship has been delayed or interrupted, any State Party in whose territory the ship or passengers or crew are present shall be bound to exercise all possible efforts to avoid a ship, its passengers, crew or cargo being unduly detained or delayed.

Article 14

Any State Party having reason to believe that an offence set forth in article 3 will be committed shall, in accordance with its national law, furnish as promptly as possible any relevant information in its possession to those States which it believes would be the States having established jurisdiction in accordance with article 6.

Article 15

1. Each State Party shall, in accordance with its national law, provide to the Secretary-General, as promptly as possible, any relevant information in its possession concerning:

   (a) the circumstances of the offence;

   (b) the action taken pursuant to article 13, paragraph 2;

   (c) the measures taken in relation to the offender or the alleged offender and, in particular, the results of any extradition proceedings or other legal proceedings.

2. The State Party where the alleged offender is prosecuted shall, in accordance with its national

law, communicate the final outcome of the proceedings to the Secretary-General.

3. The information transmitted in accordance with paragraphs 1 and 2 shall be communicated by the Secretary-General to all States Parties, to Members of the International Maritime Organization (hereinafter referred to as "the Organization"), to the other States concerned, and to the appropriate international intergovernmental organizations.

Article 16

1. Any dispute between two or more States Parties concerning the interpretation or application of this Convention which cannot be settled through negotiation within a reasonable time shall, at the request of one of them, be submitted to arbitration. If, within six months from the date of the request for arbitration, the parties are unable to agree on the organization of the arbitration any one of those parties may refer the dispute to the International Court of Justice by request in conformity with the Statute of the Court.

2. Each State may at the time of signature or ratification, acceptance or approval of this Convention or accession thereto, declare that it does not consider itself bound by any or all of the provisions of paragraph 1. The other States Parties shall not be bound by those provisions with respect to any State Party which has made such a reservation.

3. Any State which has made a reservation in accordance with paragraph 2 may, at any time, withdraw that reservation by notification to the Secretary-General.

Article 17

1. This Convention shall be open for signature at Rome on 10 March 1988 by States participating in the

International Conference on the Suppression of Unlawful Acts against the Safety of Maritime Navigation and at the Headquarters of the Organization by all States from 14 March 1988 to 9 March 1989. It shall thereafter remain open for accession.

2. States may express their consent to be bound by this Convention by:

   (a) signature without reservation as to ratification, acceptance or approval; or

   (b) signature subject to ratification, acceptance or approval, followed by ratification, acceptance or approval; or

   (c) accession.

3. Ratification, acceptance, approval or accession shall be effected by the deposit of an instrument to that effect with the Secretary-General.

Article 18

1. This Convention shall enter into force ninety days following the date on which fifteen States have either signed it without reservation as to ratification, acceptance or approval, or have deposited an instrument of ratification, acceptance, approval or accession in respect thereof.

2. For a State which deposits an instrument of ratification, acceptance, approval or accession in respect of this Convention after the conditions for entry into force thereof have been met, the ratification, acceptance, approval or accession shall take effect ninety days after the date of such deposit.

Article 19

1. This Convention may be denounced by any State Party at any time after the expiry of one year from

the date on which this Convention enters into force for that State.

2. Denunciation shall be effected by the deposit of an instrument of denunciation with the Secretary-General.

3. A denunciation shall take effect one year, or such longer period as may be specified in the instrument of denunciation, after the receipt of the instrument of denunciation by the Secretary-General.

Article 20

1. A conference for the purpose of revising or amending this Convention may be convened by the Organization.

2. The Secretary-General shall convene a conference of the States Parties to this Convention for revising or amending the Convention, at the request of one third of the States Parties, or ten States Parties, whichever is the higher figure.

3. Any instrument of ratification, acceptance, approval or accession deposited after the date of entry into force of an amendment to this Convention shall be deemed to apply to the Convention as amended.

Article 21

1. This Convention shall be deposited with the Secretary-General.

2. The Secretary-General shall:

   (a) inform all States which have signed this Convention or acceded thereto, and all Members of the Organization, of:

      (i) each new signature or deposit of an instrument of ratification, acceptance, approval or accession together with the date thereof;

(ii) the date of the entry into force of this Convention;

(iii) the deposit of any instrument of denunciation of this Convention together with the date on which it is received and the date on which the denunciation takes effect;

(iv) the receipt of any declaration or notification made under this Convention;

(b) transmit certified true copies of this Convention to all States which have signed this Convention or acceded thereto.

3. As soon as this Convention enters into force, a certified true copy thereof shall be transmitted by the Depositary to the Secretary-General of the United Nations for registration and publication in accordance with Article 102 of the Charter of the United Nations.

Article 22

This Convention is established in a single original in the Arabic, Chinese, English, French, Russian and Spanish languages, each text being equally authentic.

IN WITNESS WHEREOF: the undersigned being duly authorized by their respective Governments for that purpose have signed this Convention.

DONE AT ROME: this tenth day of March one thousand nine hundred and eighty-eight.

[1][1] Reads as "Article 7" in authentic text. Rectified 20 December 1989.

Index

Notes

Notes

Notes

Notes